An Apostate Church

Billy Lauderdale

ISBN:10: 1507511795
ISBN-13: 978-1507511794

CONTENTS

ACKNOWLEDGMENTS

What I have to say next is of the most importance, and must be understood. I'm nothing more than a simple servant of God and nothing else. I have been saved thou the blood of Christ, my lord and savior. It is God, Jesus, and the Holy Spirit, to whom I give all of the glory. For what you hold in your hands could not be if it were not for him, so it is to him that I give all of the credit and to him all of the glory.

FORWARD

What you hold in your hands is something that has came about thou many hours of prayer. It is something that God has had to deal with me about. Some may ask why He would have to deal with me about apostasy well the truth is I was in an apostate state for a while. I have now repented of my failure and turned back to God.

I have been in church for many years and felt that I was ok. When I was young I was on fire for God and was listening to Him, but as time wore on I started to listen to what man had to say instead of God. And it was that that lead me astray because I got religion. However God being who He is in His wisdom still had His hand on me. And when I began to question certain things that were preached and are believed I was always told that I was wrong. This lead to me being hurt more than once, and I began to question if I was hearing God are not. Eventually I had enough and I left the church for a little while. However God was never far from my mind I didn't worry much because I believed that I was saved because I bought into the belief, "once saved always saved" so even thou I was not in church I felt that I was ok. Finally God had enough and dealt with me let me tell you now that Is, not something that you want to go thru.

That's when God showed me that in (**Matthew 7:22:23**) *"Many will say to me in that day, Lord, Lord, have we not prophesied in thy name? And in thy name have cast out devils? And in thy name done many wonderful works? And then will I profess unto them, I never knew you: depart from me, ye that work iniquity."* Boy what an eye opener that was, He was telling me that I was not saved and went on to tell me about being in an <u>apostate</u> state of mind.

What you have here if from what God showed me about apostasy and how its effect the church and has led many to fall to the way side just like me. So my goal here is help you see that apostasy is alive and thriving in the church today and will only get worse as time goes on.

Many of you when you read this will not believe it, are say it's not in my church. And some may even have their felling hurt by what I have to say, but it's not up for debate I'm simply sharing with you what God has given me about it.

I will tell you now that if you find that this is hard for you are that it hurts your feeling you should go to God in payer and ask Him to give you the truth of the matter. And if you truly listen to God He will confirm it for you.

My prayer for you is that God will open your ears and give you eye salve so that you can hear and see what He is trying to say to you. I pray that you not harden your heart, but let Him in and turn back to him for the time that we live in is growing short.

Preface

Before sin came into the world, Adam enjoyed open communion with God; but since man separated himself from God by transgression, the human race has been cut off from this privilege. By the plan of redemption, however, a way was opened whereby the inhabitants of the earth may still have a connection with God. God has communicated with His chosen servants thou His Spirit, with divine revelation he imparted to the world His Holy Word to His chosen servants.

(**2 Peter 1:21**) "*For the prophecy came not in old time by the will of man: but holy men of God spake as they were moved by the Holy Ghost.*"

During the first twenty-five hundred years of human history, there was no written revelation. Those who had been taught of God, communicated their knowledge to others with the spoken word, and it was handed down from father to son, through successive generations. The preparation of the written word began in the time of Moses. These inspired revelations were then embodied in an inspired book. This work continued a period of sixteen hundred years—from Moses, the historian of creation and the law, to John, the recorder of the most sublime truths of the gospel.

(**2 Timothy 3:16**) "*All scripture is given by inspiration of God, and is profitable for doctrine, for reproof, for correction, for instruction in righteousness:*"

The Bible points to God as its author; yet it was written by human hands; and in the varied style of its different books it presents the characteristics of the different writers. The truths revealed can be seen in all of the Bible. For Scripture is and inspiration of God. Yet they are expressed in the words of men. The Infinite One by His Holy Spirit has shed light

3

into the minds and hearts of His servants. He has given dreams and visions, symbols and figures; and those to whom the truth was thus revealed have themselves embodied the thought in human language.

The Ten Commandments were spoken by God Himself, and were written by His own hand. They are of divine, and not of human composition. But the Bible, with its God-given truths are expressed in the language of men, this presents a union of the divine and the human. Such a union existed in the nature of Christ, who was the Son of God and the Son of man. Thus it is true of the Bible, as it was of Christ, that "*And the Word was made flesh, and dwelt among us, (and we beheld his glory, the glory as of the only begotten of the Father,) full of grace and truth.*" (**John 1:14**)

The Bible was written in different ages, by men who differed widely in rank and occupation, as well as mental and spiritual endowments, the books of the Bible present a wide contrast in style, as well as a diversity in the nature of the subjects unfolded. Different forms of expression are employed by different writers; often the same truth is more strikingly presented by one than by another. And as several writers present a subject under varied aspects and relations, there may appear, to the superficial, careless, or prejudiced reader, to be discrepancy or contradiction, where the thoughtful, reverent student, with clearer insight, can discern the underlying harmony.

As presented through different individuals, the truth is brought out in its varied aspects. One writer is more strongly impressed with one phase of the subject; he grasps those points that harmonize with his experience or with his power of perception and appreciation; another seizes upon a different phase; and each, under the guidance of the Holy Spirit, presents what is most forcibly impressed upon his own mind—a different aspect of the truth in each, but a perfect harmony through all. And the truths thus revealed unite to form a perfect whole, adapted to meet the wants of men in all the circumstances and experiences we may face in life.

God has been pleased to communicate His truth to the world by human agencies, and He Himself, by His Holy Spirit, qualified men and enabled them to do this work. He guided the mind in the selection of what to speak as well as what to write. These treasures were entrusted to earthen vessels, yet it is, nonetheless, from God. The testimony is conveyed through the imperfect expression of human language, yet it is the testimony of God; and the obedient, believing child of God beholds in it the glory of a divine power, full of grace and truth.

In His word, God has committed to men the knowledge necessary for salvation. The Holy Scriptures are to be accepted as an authoritative, infallible revelation of His will. They are the standard of character, the revealer of doctrines, and the test of experience.

(**2 Timothy 3:16-17**) *"All scripture is given by inspiration of God is profitable for doctrine, for reproof, for correction, for instruction in righteousness; That the man of God may be perfect, thoroughly furnished unto all good works."*

Yet the fact that God has revealed His will to men through His word has not rendered needless the continued presence and guiding of the Holy Spirit. On the contrary, the Spirit was promised by our Savior, to open the word to His servants, to illuminate and apply its teachings. And since it was the Spirit of God that inspired the Bible, it is impossible that the teaching of the Spirit should ever be contrary to that of the word.

The Spirit was not given—nor can it ever be bestowed— to supersede the Bible; for the Scriptures explicitly state that the word of God is the standard by which all teaching and experience must be tested. Says the apostle John.

(**1 John 4:1**) *"Beloved, believe not every spirit, but try the spirits whether they are of God: because many false prophets are gone out into the world."*

And Isaiah declares, *"To the law and to the testimony: if they speak not according to this word, it is because there is no light in them."* (**Isaiah 8:20**)

Great reproach has been cast upon the work of the Holy Spirit by the errors of a class that, claiming its enlightenment, profess to have no further need of guidance from the word of God. They are governed by impressions which they regard as the voice of God in the soul. But the spirit that controls them is not the Spirit of God. This following of impressions, to the neglect of the Scriptures, can lead only to confusion, to deception and ruin. It serves only to further the designs of the evil one. Since the ministry of the Holy Spirit is of vital importance to the church of Christ, it is one of the devices of Satan, through the errors of extremists and fanatics, to cast contempt upon the work of the Spirit and cause the people of God to neglect this source of strength which our Lord Himself has provided.

In harmony with the word of God, His Spirit was to continue its work throughout the period of the gospel dispensation. During the ages while the Scriptures of both the Old and the New Testament were being given, the Holy Spirit did not cease to communicate light to individual minds, apart from the revelations to be embodied in the Sacred Canon. The Bible itself relates how, through the Holy Spirit, men received warning, reproof, counsel, and instruction, in matters in no way relating to the giving of the Scriptures. And mention is made of prophets in different ages, of whose utterances nothing is recorded. In like manner, after the close of the canon of the Scripture, the Holy Spirit was and still to continues its work, to enlighten, warn, and comfort the children of God.

Jesus promised His disciples, *"But the Comforter, which is the Holy Ghost, whom the Father will send in My name, He shall teach you all things, and bring all things to your remembrance, whatsoever I have said unto you.*" (**John 14:26**) and again he says, "*Howbeit when He, the Spirit of truth, is come, He will guide you into all truth: for he shall not speak of himself: but whatsoever He shall hear, that shall he speak: and he will shew you things to come.*" (**John 16:13**) Scripture plainly teaches that these promises, so far from being limited to apostolic days, extend to the church of Christ in all ages. The Savior assures His followers, "*Teaching them to observe all things whatsoever I have commanded you: and, lo, I am with you always, even unto the end of the world. Amen.*" (**Matthew 28:20**) And Paul declares that the gifts and manifestations of the Spirit were set in the church "*For the perfecting of the saints, for the work of the ministry, for the edifying of the body of Christ: till we all come in the unity of the faith, and of the knowledge of the Son of God, unto a perfect man, unto the measure of the stature of the fullness of Christ.*" (**Ephesians 4:12-13**)

For the believers at Ephesus the apostle prayed, "*That the God of our Lord Jesus Christ, the Father of glory, may give unto you the Spirit of wisdom and revelation in the knowledge of Him: The eyes of your understanding being enlightened; that ye may know what is the hope of His calling, and what the riches of the glory of His inheritance in the saints, and what is the exceeding greatness if his power to us-ward who believe, according to the working of his mighty power.*" (**Ephesians 1:17-19**) The ministry of the divine Spirit in enlightening the understanding and opening to the mind the deep things of God's holy word, this was the blessing which Paul thus sought for the Ephesian church.

After the wonderful manifestation of the Holy Spirit on the Day of Pentecost, Peter exhorted the people to repentance and baptism in the name of Christ, for the remission of their sins; and he said: "*Then Peter said unto them, Repent, and be baptized every one of you in the name of Jesus Christ for the remission of sins, and Ye shall receive the gift of the Holy Ghost. For the promise is unto you, and to your children, and to all that are afar off, even as many as the Lord our God shall call.*" (**Acts 2:38-39**)

In immediate connection with the scenes of the great day of God, the Lord by the prophet Joel has promised a special manifestation of His Spirit. "*And it shall come to pass afterward, that I will pour out my sprit upon all flesh; and your sons and your daughters shall prophesy, your old men shall dream dreams, your young men shall see visions.*" (**Joel 2:28**) This prophecy received a partial fulfillment in the outpouring of the Spirit on the Day of Pentecost; but we will see it reach its full accomplishment in the manifestation of divine grace which will attend the closing work of the gospel.

The great controversy between good and evil will increase in intensity to the very close of time. In all ages the wrath of Satan has been manifested against Christ's church; and God has bestowed His grace and Spirit upon His people to strengthen them to stand against the power of the evil one. When the apostles of Christ were to bear His gospel to the world and to record it for all future ages, they were especially endowed with the enlightenment of the Spirit. But as the church approaches her final deliverance, Satan will work with greater power. He comes down *"having great wrath, because he knoweth that he hath but a short time."* (**Revelation 12:12**) He will work *"with all power and signs and lying wonders."* (**2 Thessalonians 2:9**) For six thousand years that mastermind that once was highest among the angels of God has been wholly bent to the work of deception and ruin. And all the depths of satanic skill and subtlety acquired, all the cruelty developed, during these struggles of the ages, will be brought to bear against God's people in the final conflict. And in this time of peril the followers of Christ are to bear to the world the warning of the Lord's Second Advent; and a people are to be prepared to stand before Him at His coming, *"without spot, and blameless."* (**2 Peter 3:14**) At this time the special endowment of divine grace and power is no less needed to the church than in apostolic days.

Through the illumination of the Holy Spirit, the scenes of the long-continued conflict between good and evil have been opened to the writer of these pages. From time to time I have been permitted to behold the working, in different ages, of the great controversy between Christ, the Prince of life, the Author of our salvation, and Satan, the prince of evil, the author of sin, and the first transgressor of God's holy law. Satan's enmity against Christ has been manifested against His followers. The same hatred of the principles of God's law, the same policy of deception, by which error is made to appear as truth, by which human laws are substituted for the law of God, and men are led to worship the creature rather than the Creator, may be traced in all the history of the past. Satan's efforts to misrepresent the character of God, to cause men to cherish a false conception of the Creator, and thus to regard Him with fear and hate rather than with love; his endeavors to set aside the divine law, leading the people to think themselves free from its requirements; and his persecution of those who dare to resist his deceptions, have been steadfastly pursued in all ages. They may be traced in the history of the patriarchs, prophets, and apostles, and of martyrs and reformers.

In the great final conflict, Satan will employ the same policy, manifest the same spirit, and work for the same end as in all preceding ages. That which has been, will be, except that the coming struggle will be marked with a terrible intensity such as the world has never witnessed. Satan's deceptions will be more subtle, his assaults more determined. If it were possible, he would lead astray the elect.

(**1 John 4:1**) *"For false Christ and false prophets shall rise, and shall shew sings and wonders, to seduce, if it were possible, even the elect."*

7

As the Spirit of God has opened to my mind the great truths of His word, and the scenes of the past and the future, I have been bidden to make known to others that which has thus been revealed and especially so to present it as to shed a light on the fast-approaching struggle of the future. In pursuance of this purpose, I have endeavored to select and group together certain things in the church in such a manner as to trace the unfolding of the great testing truths that, have excited the wrath of Satan, and the enmity of a world-loving church, and that have been maintained by the witness of those who "loved not their lives unto the death."

It is my hope that in these words we may see a foreshadowing of the conflict before us. Regarding them in the light of God's word, and by the illumination of His Spirit, we may see unveiled the devices of the wicked one, and the dangers which they must shun who would be found "without fault" before the Lord at His coming.

The great events which have marked the progress of reform in past ages are matters of history, well known and universally acknowledged by the Protestant world; they are facts which none can gainsay. This I have presented briefly, in accordance with the scope of the book, and the brevity which must necessarily be observed, the facts having been condensed into as little space as seemed consistent with a proper understanding of their application. In some cases where so grouped together as to afford, in brief, a comprehensive view of the subject, or has summarized details in a convenient manner, words have been quoted; but in some instances no specific credit has been given, since the quotations are not given for the purpose of citing that writer as authority, but because his statement affords a ready and forcible presentation of the subject. In narrating the experience and views of those carrying forward the work of reform in our own time, similar use has been made of their works.

It is not so much the object of this book to present new truths concerning the struggles of former times, as to bring out facts and principles which have a bearing on coming events. Yet viewed as a part of the controversy between the forces of light and darkness, all these records are seen to have a new significance; and through them a light is cast upon the future, illumining the pathway of those who, like the reformers of past ages, will be called, even at the peril of all earthly good, to witness "for the word of God, and for the testimony of Jesus Christ."

To unfold the scenes of the great controversy between truth and error; to reveal the wiles of Satan, and the means by which he may be successfully resisted; to present a satisfactory solution of the great problem of evil, shedding such a light upon the origin and the final disposition of sin as to make fully manifest the justice and benevolence of God in all His dealings with His creatures; and to show the holy, unchanging nature of His law, is the object of this book. That through its influence souls may be delivered from the power of darkness, and become "partakers of the inheritance of the saints in light," to the praise of Him who loved us, and gave Himself for us, is the earnest prayer.

1Apostasy

Question: "What is apostasy and how can I recognize it?"

Answer: Apostasy, from the Greek word *apostasia*, means "a defiance of an established system or authority; a rebellion; an abandonment or breach of faith." In the first-century world, apostasy was a technical term for political revolt or defection. And just like in the first century, apostasy threatens the Body of Christ today.

The Bible warns about people like Arius (c. A.D. 250 - 336), a Christian priest from Alexandria, Egypt, who was trained at Antioch in the early fourth century. About A.D. 318, Arius accused Bishop Alexander of Alexandria of subscribing to Sabellianism, a false teaching which asserted that the Father, Son, and Holy Spirit were merely roles or modes assumed by God at various times. Arius was determined to emphasize the oneness of God; however, he went too far in his teaching of God's nature. Arius denied the Trinity and introduced what appeared on the surface to be an inconsequential difference between the Father and Son.

Arius argued that Jesus was not *homoousios* (of the same essence) as the Father, but was rather *homoiousios* (of similar essence). Only one Greek letter – the iota (I) – separated the two. Arius described his position in this manner: "The Father existed before the Son. There was a time when the Son did not exist. Therefore, the Son was created by the Father. Therefore, although the Son was the highest of all creatures, he was not of the essence of God."

Arius was very clever and did his best to get the people on his side, even going so far as to compose little songs that taught his theology, which he tried to teach to everyone who would listen. His winsome nature and revered position as a preacher and one who lived in denial of himself contributed also to his cause.

With respect to apostasy, it is critical that all Christians understand two important things:

(1) How to recognize apostasy and apostate teachers.
(2) Why apostate teaching is so deadly.

The Forms of Apostasy

To fully identify and combat apostasy, it is important that Christians understand its various forms and the traits that characterize its doctrines and teachers. As to the forms of apostasy, there are two main types:

(1) A falling away from key and true doctrines of the Bible into heretical teachings that proclaim to be "the real" Christian doctrine.
(2) A complete renunciation of the Christian faith, which results in a full abandonment of Christ.

Arius represents the first form of apostasy—a denial of key Christian truths (such as the divinity of Christ) that begins a downhill slide into a full departure from the faith, which is the second form of apostasy. It is important to understand that the second form almost always begins with the first. A heretical belief becomes a heretical teaching that splinters and grows until it pollutes all aspects of a person's faith, and then the end goal of Satan is accomplished, which is a complete falling away from Christianity.

A recent example of this process is a 2010 study done by prominent atheist Daniel Dennett and Linda LaScola called "Preachers Who Are Not Believers." Dennett and LaScola's work chronicles five different preachers who over time were presented with and accepted heretical teachings about Christianity and now have completely fallen away from the faith and are either pantheists or clandestine atheists. One of the most disturbing truths highlighted in the study is that these preachers maintain their position as pastors of Christian churches with their congregations being unaware of their leader's true spiritual state.

The dangers of apostasy were warned about in the book of Jude, which serves as a handbook for understanding the characteristics of apostates like those chronicled in Dennett and LaScola's study. Jude's words are every bit as relevant for us today as they were when he penned them in the first century, so it is important we carefully read and understand them.

The Characteristics of Apostasy and Apostates

Jude was the half-brother of Jesus and a leader in the early church. In his New Testament letter, he outlines how to recognize apostasy and strongly urges those in the body of Christ to contend earnestly for the faith.

(**Jude 1:3**) *"Beloved, when I gave all diligence to write unto you of the common salvation, it was needful for me to write unto you, and exhort you that ye should earnestly contend for the faith which was once delivered unto the saints."*

The Greek word translated "contend earnestly" is a compound verb from which we get the word "agonize." It is in the present infinitive form, which means that the struggle will be continuous. In other words, Jude is telling us that there will be a constant fight against false teaching and that Christians should take it so seriously that we "agonize" over the fight in which we are engaged. Moreover, Jude makes it clear that every Christian is called to this fight, not just church leaders, so it is critical that all believers sharpen their discernment skills so that they can recognize and prevent apostasy in their midst.

After urging his readers to contend earnestly for the faith, Jude highlights the reason:

(**Jude 1:4**) *"For there are certain men crept in unawares, who were before of old ordained to this condemnation, ungodly men, turning the grace of our God into licentiousness, and denying the only Lord God, and our Lord Jesus Christ."*

In this one verse, Jude provides Christians with three traits of apostasy and apostate teachers.

First, Jude says that apostasy can be subtle. Jude uses the word "crept" (found in no other book of the Bible) to describe the apostate's entry into the church. In extra-biblical Greek, the term describes the cunning craftiness of a lawyer who, through clever argumentation, infiltrates the minds of courtroom officials and corrupts their thinking. The word literally means "slip in sideways; come in stealthily; sneak in; hard to detect." In other words, Jude says it is rare that apostasy begins in an overt and easily detectable manner. Instead, it looks a lot like Arius' preaching in which, in a nonchalant manner, only a single letter differentiates his doctrine from the real teaching of the Christian faith.

Describing this aspect of apostasy and its underlying danger, so skilled is error at imitating truth, that the two are constantly being mistaken for each another. It takes a sharp eye these days to know which brother is Cain and which is Abel. The apostle Paul also speaks to the outwardly pleasing behavior of apostates and their teaching when he says, *"For such men are false apostles, deceitful workers, transforming themselves as apostles of Christ. And no marvel; for Satan himself is transformed into an angel of light."* (**2 Corinthians 11:13-14**) In other words, do not look for apostates to appear bad on the outside or speak dramatic words of heresy at the outset of their teaching. Rather than denying truth outright, apostates will twist it to fit their own agenda, but as pastor R. C. Lensky has noted, "The worst forms of wickedness consist in perversions of the truth."

Second, Jude describes the apostates as "ungodly" and as those who use God's grace as a license to commit unrighteous acts. Beginning with "ungodly," Jude describes fourteen unflattering traits of apostates so his readers can more easily identify them. See the book of Jude:

(1) Jude says the apostates are ungodly men (**Jude 1:4**)
(2) Turning the grace of our God into lasciviousness (**Jude 1:4**)
(3) denying the only Lord God (**Jude 1:4**)
(4) filthy dreamers defile the flesh (**Jude 1:8**)
(5) despise dominion (**Jude 1:8**)
(6) speak evil of dignities (**Jude 1:8**)
(7) speak evil of those things which they know not (**Jude 1:10**)
(8) corrupt themselves (**Jude 1:10**)
(9) complainers (**Jude 1:16**)
(10) walking after their own lusts (**Jude 1:16**)
(11) their mouth speaketh great swelling words (**Jude 1:16**)
(12) mockers in the last time (**Jude 1:18**)
(13) they who separate themselves (**Jude 1:19**)
(14) having not the Spirit (**Jude 1:19**)

Third, Jude says apostates "deny our only Master and Lord, Jesus Christ." How do apostates do this? Paul tells us in his letter to Titus. (**Titus 1:15-16**) "*Unto the pure, all things are pure; but unto those that are defiled and unbelieving, is nothing pure; but even their mind and their conscience is defiled. They profess to know God; but in works they deny Him, being abominable, and disobedient, and unto every good work reprobate.*" Through their unrighteous behavior, the apostates show their true selves. Unlike an apostate, a true believer is someone who has been delivered from sin to righteousness in Christ. With Paul, they ask the apostates who promote licentious behavior.

(**Romans 6:1-2**) "*What shall we say then? Shall we continue in sin that grace may abound? God forbid. How shall we, that are dead to sin, live any longer therein?*"

But the apostates' false teaching also shows their true nature. Peter says, "*But there were false prophets also arose among the people, even as there shall be false teachers among you, who privily shall bring in damnable heresies, even denying the Lord that bought them, and bring upon themselves swift destruction.*" (**2 Peter 2:1**) Another aspect of true believers is that they have been delivered out of spiritual darkness into light see (**Ephesians 5:8**) and therefore will not deny core truths of Scripture like Arius did with the divinity of Jesus.

Ultimately, the sign of an apostate is that he eventually falls away and departs from the truth of God's Word and His righteousness. The apostle John signifies this is a mark of a false believer: *"They went out from us, but they were not of us; for if they had been of us, they would no doubt have continued with us: but they went out, that they might be made manifest that they were not all of us."* (**1 John 2:19**)

Ideas Have Consequences

That God takes apostasy and false teaching seriously is evidenced by the fact that every New Testament book except Philemon contains warnings about false teaching. Why is this simply because ideas have consequences? Right thinking and its fruit produces goodness, whereas wrong thinking and its accompanying action results in undesired penalties. As an example, the Cambodian killing fields in the 1970s were the product of the nihilistic worldview of Jean Paul Sartre and his teaching. The Khmer Rouge's leader Pol Pot lived out Sartre's philosophy toward the people in a clear and frightening way, which was articulated in this manner: "To keep you is no benefit. To destroy you is no loss."

It should be remembered that Satan did not come to the first couple in the Garden with an external armament or supernatural weapon; instead, he came to them with an idea. And it was that idea that condemned them and the rest of humankind, with the only remedy being the sacrificial death of God's Son.

The great tragedy is, whether knowingly or unknowingly, the apostate teacher dooms his unsuspecting followers. One of the most frightening verses in all of Scripture comes from the lips of Jesus. Speaking to His disciples about the religious leaders of His day, He said.

(**Matthew 15:14**) *"Let them alone: they be blind leaders of the blind. And if the blind lead the blind, both will fall into the ditch."*

This verse is alarming because Jesus affirms that it is not only the false teachers that go to destruction, but their disciples who also follow them. Christian philosopher Soren Kierkegaard put it this way: "For it has never yet been known to fail that one fool, when he goes astray, takes several others with him."

Conclusion

In A.D. 325, the Council of Nicene convened primarily to take up the issue of Arius and his teaching. Much to Arius's dismay, the end result was his excommunication and a statement in the Nicene Creed that affirmed Christ's divinity: "We believe in one God, the Father Almighty, maker of all things visible and invisible; and in one Lord Jesus Christ, the Son of God, the only-begotten of his Father, of the substance of the Father, God of God, Light of Light, very God of very God, begotten not made, being of one substance with the Father."

Arius may have died centuries ago, but his spiritual children are still with us to this day in the form of cults like the Jehovah's Witnesses and others who deny Christ's true essence and person. Sadly, until Christ returns and every last spiritual enemy has been removed, tares such as these will be present among the wheat see (**Matthew 13:24-30**). In fact, Scripture says apostasy will only get worse as Christ's return approaches.

(**Matthew 24:10**) "*And then shall* [the latter days] *many be offended, and shall betray one another, and shall hate one another.*"

Paul echoes Jesus in his inspired writings as well. The apostle told the Thessalonians that a great falling away would precede Christ's second coming see (**2 Thessalonians 2:3**) and that the end times would be characterized by tribulation and hollow religious charlatans:

(**2 Timothy 3:1-5**) "*This know also, that in the last days perilous times shall come. For men shall be lovers of their own selves, covetous, boasters, proud, blasphemers, disobedient to parents, unthankful, unholy, Without natural affection, trucebreakers, false accusers, incontinent, fierce, despisers of those that are good, Traitors, heady, highminded, lovers of pleasure more than lovers of God; having a form of godliness, but denying the power thereof: from such turn away.*"

It is critical, now more than ever, that every believer prays for discernment, to combat apostasy, and contend earnestly for the faith that has once and for all been delivered to the saints.

Apostasy has taken over the church and Christians today

Apostasy includes two types:

(1) Those who have knowingly turned completely from Jesus Christ and no longer even pretend to be Christians.
(2) Those who still claim to be Christians but have departed from the faith (the great faith).

The latter (2) can be divided in to three areas:

(1) Those Christians who have taken the world and mixed it with the church resulting too weak, little or no faith in Jesus Christ.

(2) Those who have deliberately twisted the scriptures perverting the word of God to fit their circumstances and pursue what they want to. This include the Christians, the teachers, the pastors and all men of God who are searching for a share of power, fame and money; scoffers preaching what people want to hear so not to offend anyone.

(3) The naive, who are genuinely deceived by false men of Satan, dressed in sheep clothes.

Paul was dealing much on the apostasy in the early church; the correction of false doctrine and practice that was already in the early church in the days of the apostles.

Apostasy in the End Time

The bible points at the apostasy too be a sign of the last days, the End Time. And yes, I believe here we are.

When Jesus was asked by His disciples, *"And as he sat upon the mount of Olives, the disciples came unto him privately, saying, Tell us, when shall these things be? And what shall be the sign of thy coming and of the end of the world."* (**Matthew 24:3**) The first words were *"And Jesus answered and said unto them, take heed that no man deceive you."* (**Matthew 24:4**)

In His response, He emphasized religious deception three times and He specified what it would involve: (**Matthew 4-5, 11**)

(**Matthew 24:4-5**) *"And Jesus answered and said unto them, Take heed that no man deceive you. For many shall come in my name, saying, I am Christ; and shall deceive many."*

(**Matthew 24:11**) *"And many false prophets shall rise, and shall deceive many."*

(**Matthew 24:24**) *"For there shall arise false Christ's, and false prophets, and shall shew great signs and wonders; insomuch that if it were possible, they shall deceive the very elect."*

Jude puts it straight and clear

(**Jude 1:3-4**) *"Beloved, when I gave all diligence to write unto you of the common salvation, it was needful for me to write unto you, and exhort you that ye should earnestly contend for the faith which was once delivered unto the saints. For there are certain men crept in unawares, who were before of old ordained to this condemnation, ungodly men, turning the grace of our God into lasciviousness, and denying the only Lord God, and our Lord Jesus Christ."*

These ungodly men are inside the church today, perverting and twisting each and every doctrine of Christianity and deceiving many. We have to be careful and expose them so that our faith and the faith of others might not be swayed.

If there is indeed an apostasy occurring in the Christian Church, we would not know it unless we first examined the Bible (the truth) and then compared the Church to the Word of God. It is only after truth is established that we would have a measuring rod by which apostasy can be detected.

2 THE SIGNS OF THE TIMES

The Great revolt

When we read some of the things that Jesus said it's as though He were reading from the news summary of recent years, His prophecies of two thousand years ago clearly describe our times. Thus, we are compelled to discern accurately the significance of the era in which we live. Indeed, of the many prophetic fulfillments of our day, one in particular rises with undimmed candor. I am speaking of what the Bible calls the "apostasy." Recall Paul's warning:

(**2 Thessalonians 2:3**)"*Let no man deceive you by any manes; for that day shall not come, except there come a falling away first, and the man of sin be revealed, the son of perdition;*"

Apostasy has traditionally been described as a time of deception and massive falling away from authentic faith in Christ. If you will take the time to look at the church you can see that apostasy is occurring. Depending upon your specific view, sometime before or after the apostasy the rapture of the church will occur. However, the concept of apostasy as merely "a falling away" is incomplete. The original Greek word for apostasy, *apostasia*, when used in classical Greek literature, meant "a political revolt." From this we understand that the end-time apostasy is not just a time of sinfulness or large scale backsliding; it is actually a time of open defiance and warlike aggression against godliness in general. In other words, the apostasia is a political insurrection against the laws of God.

This interpretation of the apostasy is not an isolated view. The New International Version, Revised Standard Version, Phillips Translation, and New English Bible all render *apostasia* as "the rebellion." The Living Bible interprets the apostasy as the "great rebellion," while the Jerusalem Bible assigns a proper name to this era: "The Great Revolt."

As we consider the fulfillment of so many other prophecies, let us carefully observe: mankind has entered an era of open revolt and outright rebellion -- an apostasy -- against the moral standards of God. This can be seen in almost every church and every country and its only going to grow worse as time goes on.

Today, we are witnessing a large-scale rebellion against traditional moral values. Indeed, this brazen attitude has had a name for itself since the 1960s: such as the sexual revolution. And "revolution" is exactly what it is. Our moral standards have not only been challenged, they have been replaced by a nonstandard. Indeed, the great rebellion seeks to legitimize and then mainstream every perversity known to man! It can best be seen with the open acceptance of homosexually in the pulpit, with ordained ministers. And in the way sin is tolerated in the church.

There is much to say on behalf of those trapped in perversity and who hate sin's affect on their lives. We must be compassionate toward them and not strident; many are sitting in our churches afraid to even speak of their need lest they be disowned. I am not speaking with reference to the victims of this advance, but of those who are engaged in a mutiny against the sway of God in our nation. They argue the only standard Americans have is the standard of individual freedom. In their view, freedom itself is the "god" ruling America, with self-indulgence sitting as prime minister.

Yet the God of Heaven desires the nations of the world to turn to Him. Though the apostasy will certainly intensify, we must remember it is only one of many prophecies unfolding in our day. The same divine Word that warned of the Great Rebellion also assures us that ultimately God's kingdom shall crush the demonic influences in our world.

(**Daniel 2:44**) *"And in the days of these kings shall the God of heaven set up a kingdom, which shall never be destroyed: and the kingdom shall not be left to other people, but it shall break in pieces and consume all these kingdoms, and it shall stand for ever".*

Yes, evil shall mature into full rebellion, but good is also ripening into full Christ likeness! See (**Matthew 13:40-43; John 17:22-23**) True, the apostasy shall reveal the nature of Satan, but the true church shall manifest the nature of Christ! Our King is not only coming in the skies, He is coming.

(**2 Thessalonians 1:10**) *"When he shall come to be glorified in His saints, and to be admired in all them that believe (because our testimony among you was believed) in that day."*

What seems to be Satan's hour, full of darkness and rebellion, is simply the opportunity for grace to abound to the glory of God in the church!

Seated with Christ

The Second Psalm, perhaps more than any other Bible text, accurately portrays the spirit of our time. Indeed, it also proclaims our correct response to Satan's bold advance. Although it was quoted by the early church, see (**Acts 4:25-26**) God has set its full realization for the end of this age.

(**Psalm 2:1-3**) "*Why do the heathen rage, and the people imagine a vain thing? The kings of the earth set themselves, and the rulers take counsel together, against the LORD, and against His anointed, saying, 'Let us their bands asunder, and cast away their cords from us.*"

Although "the rebellion" reveals itself worldwide in many ways, in America many of our leaders have certainly been counseling together "against the Lord" in their decisions. We see it in the efforts to mainstream perversion and give shelter to satanic things. Again, our anti-censorship laws, like armor plating, in many ways now defend sin against the Lord. The virulent cry of those in rebellion hammers relentlessly upon the fetters of moral restraint!

He who sits in the heavens laughs

This railing against God has not gone unnoticed in Heaven. Is the Almighty confounded? Has fear concerning recent developments gripped the Lord's heart? No. The Psalm continues:

(**Psalm 2:4-5**) "*He that sitteth in the heavens shall laugh: the Lord shall them in derision. Then shall he speak unto them in his wrath, and vex them in His sore displeasure.*"

The Lord laughs at the foolishness of those in full revolt, as they imagine God's judgments cannot reach them. Why then, you ask, does the Lord delay His full judgment? In part, the Lord waits for us, His church. For while the world shall demand, and receive, the reign of hell, the goal of the praying church shall be for the reign of Heaven.

You see, *all* prophecies shall be fulfilled: not only those concerning evil but also those concerning righteousness. The Lord has purposed to have a "*bride without spot or wrinkle*" and a "kingdom" of wheat without tares. The transformation of the church will be fulfilled as surely as every other prophecy occurring before the Lord's return.

Thus, with great fear and holy trembling, we must review what God has promised concerning us. Let us remember, the Lord is not alone in the heavens. According to His Word, He has "*And hath raised us up together, and made us sit together in the heavenly places in Christ Jesus:*" (**Ephesians 2:6**) it is time for our identity as Christians to shift. Our nationalities only define our ambassador status; our true citizenship is in Heaven.

(**Philippians 3:20**) *"For our conversation is in heaven; from whence also we look for the Saviour, the Lord Jesus Christ."*

And if God is laughing at the mocking of those in the rebellion, let us also, as His subjects, share His confidence!

Thus, He commands us to sit with Him in the completeness of His purpose. He requires us not only to live without fear but to stand in prayer for these very nations that defy Him!

Listen again to this Second Psalm, for in the very context of worldwide rebellion against the Lord, it records the most remarkable discourse:

(**Psalms 2:8**) "*Ask of Me, and I shall give thee the heathen for thine inheritance, and the uttermost parts of the earth for thy possession.*"

When I first came to Christ in the 70's, churches in America were deeply divided and rather cold in organized prayer. Today, leaders of denominations are working together, and it is estimated that more than a quarter of a million American churches are moving toward deeper unity and increased prayer for this nation. Jesus has asked the Father for the United States, and in response, the prayer movement has been born!

As Christ's church, we do not deserve a national revival, but Jesus does! As His representatives, in His name and virtue, we ask of the Father for America! We stand in prayer for the church to become one, filled with Christ followers from every ethnic background! Our prayer is not only an act of faith; it is an act of obedience: we are commanded to ask God for the nations!

Therefore, while the perverse strive toward complete rejection of God, even as their mocking words fill the air, the Almighty's unchangeable promise to His Son (and by extension, His church as Christ's body) is "*Ask of Me, and I will surely give the nations!*"

As violence, New Age religions and witchcraft flourish in our schools, ask God for this nation. While all restraint is removed from the entertainment industry, ask God for this nation! While perversity dresses in normalcy, ask God for America! While abortion remains protected by laws, ask God with confidence, with boldness, and with faith for our land! Where you see injustice in any form, ask God for His kingdom to manifest on earth!

Put away fear and discouragement; repent of fretting. The more we accept our place in the divine plan, the more we shall laugh at the enemy's plans. The faith that relentlessly asks God pleases God. Now, as the fullness of the times unfolds, as the world around us clothes itself in prophetic fulfillments, let us put away unbelief; let us repent for withdrawal. It is a time to boldly ask of God. As He has promised: He will give the nations as an inheritance to Christ!

Proof of the fact

(**Matthew 24:14**) "*And this gospel of the kingdom shall be preached in all the world for a witness unto all nations; and then shall the end come.*"

Many in the church today try to determine the nearness of Christ's return by reading the signs of the times. We see such signs in specific events; for example, the return of the Jews to Israel. Yet one of the clearest statements Jesus makes about His second coming is contained in the verse above. The end will come only after the gospel has been preached to all nations-as a testimony.

The word that Jesus uses for "witness" in this verse is the same Greek word used for "testimony." It means, literally, "proof of the fact." Christ is speaking here of not just preaching the gospel, but presenting it as a testimony. In short, He says the gospel we preach is effective only if it is backed up by a life that testifies to its reality.

Never before in the history of the world have there been the opportunity are the ability to spread the witness of Christ like we have now. With TV and the internet it can spread at almost the speed of light.

You would think that in America, a nation filled with thousands of evangelical churches, there would be a strong gospel witness. But many churches have compromised the true gospel of Christ. The fact is, even with all the evangelical preaching in many of these churches, there is very little testimony of Christ's lordship in the people's lives to back it up. They are not a true witness to the city or the nation.

Of course, there are exceptions however they are getting hard to find. I heard a story of a pastor who at one time planned to build a new church building. His congregation was growing rapidly and he had been studying the church-growth movement. But his wife was stirred to pray and seek the Lord, and soon the pastor was doing the same. He quickly gave up his dream of huge numbers and began to be a testimony of what he preached.

He told his congregation, "God´s Spirit has been speaking to me about the sins of this church. The pastor then listed sin after sin fornication, adultery, alcoholism, drug abuse, pornography. Then he began his sermon: "We´re not about to start building a big church right now. We´ve got to get Christ´s living tabernacle straightened out before we can do anything else. We have to live this gospel first!" He heard from God he knew that first they must live the gospel. Today the Spirit of God is moving mightily in that church. People are flocking to the Lord, getting their lives straight- because they are hearing a gospel and seeing a living testimony behind it!

Today too many Christians have lost their hunger for God. Instead of coming into the Lord's presence hungry for more of His fullness, our thoughts are held hostage to worldly pursuits and fleshly distractions. At best we are merely curious about spiritual realities, but not truly hungry.

Let us look at a few vital Scriptures. See (**Acts 15:1-29**) This whole passage is about a great meeting of the apostles to decide whether - with the new Gentile Christians – it was "*necessary to circumcise them and to command them to keep the Law of Moses.*" (**Acts 15:5**) So what did the apostles conclude about this? As Peter declared during the debate about it, "*Now therefore why tempt ye God, to put a yoke upon the neck of the disciples, which neither our fathers nor we were able to bear?*" (**Acts 15:10**)

At the end of the great meeting, the apostles put out a letter to the Gentile Christians that declared:

(**Acts 15:28-29**) "*For it seemed good to the Holy Ghost, and to us, to lay upon you no greater burden than these necessary things: that you abstain from meats offered to idols, and from blood, and from things strangled, and from fornication: from which if ye keep yourselves, ye shall do well. Fare ye well.*"

And as far as they were concerned, that was it! In other words, no "Torah observance", no Sabbath, no circumcision, no Old Law apart from these few things this brief list only. That was the pronouncement of the apostles. If they wanted to tell the Gentiles anything else then this was the place to do it. But it is definitely not included. And neither are a thousand-and-one other thing's from the Old Testament.

Of course, this should be no surprise to us. In (**Colossians 2**), Paul tells us very clearly that Christ has "wiped out the handwriting of requirements that was against us" by nailing it to the cross (Verse 14). He then goes on to say:

(**Colossians 2:16-17**) "*Let no man therefore judge you in meat, or in drink, or respect of an holyday, or of the new moon, or of the Sabbath days: which are a shadow of things to come; but the body of Christ.*"

So all those Old Testament practices were only a "shadow" of the New, In fact, as Hebrews makes clear, the entire Old Covenant was only a 'type' or shadow of that which was to come. It was not the real thing! It does not make us more "holy"! The substance is found in Christ - and Him alone. The Old Torah "requirements" were nailed to the cross with Jesus. We don't need them anymore. If anybody ever tells you that the New Testament is simply a "continuation" of the Old, and we must follow them run a mile from that person. They simply do not know what they are talking about. In fact, what they are spouting is dangerous heresy. Note here we are not to do away with the Old Testament it is a part of the word of God, but we are not to hold the old laws and restrictions that they but on us.

So we do not "have" to observe the old laws. It does not make us more 'holy' or righteous to do so. It is simply a matter of conscience. This runs against a lot of the teaching that is going around right now. There is a lot of dangerous teaching that is bringing a lot of harm to a lot of people. Many of them don't even realize what is happening to them.

Paul clearly tells us in Galatians that you can lose your salvation by beginning to rely on the Law in your Christian walk:

(**Galatians 4:10-11**) "*Ye observe days, and months and times, and years. I am afraid for you, lest I have labor in vain*"

He then goes on to say, "*Christ is become of no effect unto you, whosoever of you are justified by the Law; ye are fallen from grace.*" (**Galatians 5:4**) Alarming statements, are they not?

You see, it is a direct insult to the work of Christ and to God for us to go back to the "works of the Law" to try and make us more 'righteous' in His sight. It is placing our trust in something other than just Jesus. We are "adding works" for our salvation. And it will not do.

I believe that just like the Galatians, a lot of people today need to repent of trying to add the Old Law to their salvation – sometimes in subtle ways - sometimes major. This is not the kind of thing to toy around with. It can be utterly deadly. If you are someone who is adding to your faith, I urge you to repent.

The Sphere of New Life

We seek to show, by a few examples, the boundless range and scope of one brief phrase of two or three short words: *in Christ*, or, *in Christ Jesus*. A very small key may open a very complex lock and a very large door, and that door may itself lead into a vast building with priceless stores of wealth and beauty. This brief phrase -- a preposition followed by a proper name -- is the key to the whole New Testament.

Those three short words, *in Christ Jesus*, are, without doubt, the most important ever written, even by an inspired pen, to express the mutual relation of the believer and Christ. They occur, with their equivalents, over one hundred and thirty times. Sometimes we meet the expression, *in Christ* or *in Christ Jesus*, and ... sometimes this sacred name, or its equivalent pronoun, is found associated with other prepositions -- through, with, by; but the thought is essentially the same. Such repetition and variety must have some intense meaning. When, in the Word of God, a phrase like this occurs so often, and with such manifold applications, it cannot be a matter of accident; there is a deep design. God's Spirit is bringing a truth of the highest importance before us, repeating for the sake of emphasis, compelling even the careless reader to give heed as to some vital teaching.

If there be one truth of the Gospel that is fundamental, and underlies all else, it is this: A new life in Christ Jesus. He, Himself, clearly and forcibly expressed it in:

(**John 15:4**) "*Abide in me, and I in you. As the branch cannot bear fruit of itself, except it abide in the vine; no more can ye, except ye abide in me.*"

By a matchless parable our Lord there taught us that all believers are branches of the Living Vine, and that, apart from Him we are nothing and can do nothing because we have in us no life. This truth finds expression in many ways in the Holy Scripture, but most frequently in that short and simple phrase we are now considering -- *in Christ Jesus*.

Such a phrase suggests that He is to the believer the sphere of this new life or being. Let us observe -- a sphere rather than a circle. A circle surrounds us, but only on one plane; but a sphere encompasses and envelopes us, surrounding us in every direction and on every plane. If you draw a circle on the floor, and step within its circumference, you are within it only on the level of the floor. But, if that circle could become a sphere, and you are within it, it would on every side surround you -- above and below, before and behind, on the right hand and on the left. Moreover, the sphere that surrounds you also separates you from whatever is outside of it. Again, in proportion as such a sphere is strong it also protects whatever is within it from all that is without -- from all external foes or perils. And yet again, it supplies, to whomsoever is within it, whatever it contains. This may help us to understand the great truth taught with such clearness, especially in the New Testament. Christ is there presented throughout as the sphere of the believer's whole life and being, and in this truth are included these conditions:

(1)　First, Christ Jesus surrounds or embraces the believer, in His own life;

(2) Second, He separates the believer in Himself from all hostile influences;
(3) Third, He protects him in Himself from all perils and foes of his life;
(4) Fourth, He provides and supplies in Himself all that is needful.

The more we study the phrase [*in Christ Jesus*] and the various instances and peculiar varieties of such recurrence, the more shall we be convinced of its vital importance to all practical holy living. (May everyone who repents and receives Christ as personal Lord and Savior take great consolation in being "in Christ Jesus").

The seeds of apostasy

John Wesley recounted that within every revival were the seeds of apostasy. By this he meant that with revival came righteousness, with righteousness came favor, with favor came prosperity, and with prosperity came the temptation of self-reliance. This temptation of self-reliance is the first step away from God. It is sad that people are willing to serve the illusion of prosperity by means of self-reliance.

As Americans we can definitely see how this insight fits our country. Our land was birthed with the ideal that a nation should have the freedom to worship the true and living God according to one's conscience. The Almighty had blessed our nation with righteousness. With righteousness came national favor, with favor came prosperity, and now we, as a nation, bear the burdens of decline resulting from our own self-reliance. As American Christians we can see how the Spirit of the Lord could speak of a church that sees itself as *"increased of goods and have need of nothing"*. (**Revelation 3:17**)

When idolatry's seed of self-reliance yields its crop perversion, poverty, and struggle will always follow—many who claim to be worshippers of Almighty God will turn to other gods. These gods are the gods which originate in the satanically manipulated carnal heart. These gods are conceived in the human imagination and constructed by human hands. These gods of imagery are bombarding Americans now, seducing us in a downward spiral of the media's ongoing promotion of abomination against God.

Our present "it's the economy" or "its health care" politicians have replaced Jeremiah's prosperity prophets, giving us a false sense of security by proclaiming blessing and peace upon the land. Our "soft-sell" preachers are proclaiming health and wealth, while the glory is preparing to depart from our places of worship. "Change that makes a difference" will not come by the hands of men. "Change that will make a difference" will only come when we cast our idols down at the foot of the cross.

Where are the believers like Ezekiel today? Where are the watchmen on the wall of a nation's destiny—crying out that the enemy is coming, that the glory is lifting, and that God is turning His back?

Political correctness tells us not to speak in such a manner. Religious convenience tells us not to prophecy such, for the people have ears that need to be tickled.

(**2 Timothy 4:3**) *"For the time will come when they will not endure sound doctrine; but after their own lusts shall they heap to themselves teachers, having itching ears."*

As a passionate believer, I cannot help but speak a word of warning. As a passionate oracle of the truth, I must speak the promise of restoration and grace in order that many may be given the opportunity to cast down their idols and return to the God of our fathers.

The harness of the Lord

There is a terrific operation of the Spirit going on today to bring the Sons of God into an absolute confinement to the perfect will of God. This is the Day of His perfection, the day in which He is preparing the channel through which He shall pour forth His Glory for the entire world to see. This channel is His Body in the earth, that glorious company of people who are being conformed through much tribulation and fiery tests to the image of the Son of God... The weapons of their warfare are not carnal, natural weapons, but they are mighty weapons, mighty through God to the pulling down of strongholds. These are those who shall "be strong and do exploits."

But before God can commit this great and tremendous ministry into their hands, they must submit themselves to the discipline of the Lord, letting Him truly be the Lord of their entire lives. We have long since dealt with the question of open sin, but now God is dealing with the inward rebellion of our own wills. Some good Christians are not now being so dealt with, for they are not in this First fruits Company, but nevertheless there is a real dealing of God going on within those who are called into the High Calling of God. This is a very real thing, and is the work of the Refiner's Fire. To those who are going through it, some of its aspects are horrible, but very necessary, and the end result thereof is glorious as we are brought into absolute and complete submission to the will of our Lord.

While we were children, young and undisciplined, limited only by the outer fence of our understanding and ran around the limits of the pastures (that kept us from getting into the dark pastures of poison weeds), He was content to watch us develop into young manhood, spiritually speaking. But the time has came to those who have fed in His pastures, and drank from His streams, when they were to be brought into the discipline or "child training" for the purpose of making them mature sons to put on the harness of His guidance. Many of the children today cannot understand why some of those who have put on the harness of God cannot get excited by the many religious games and the playful antics of the immature. They wonder why the disciplined ones run not after every new revelation or feed on every opportunity to engage in seemingly "good and profitable" religious activities. They wonder why some will not race with them in their frantic effort to build great works and great and notable ministries. They cannot understand the simple fact that this company of saints is waiting for the voice of the Master, and they do not hear God in all this outward activity. They will move in their time, when the Master speaks. But not before, though many temptations come. And they cannot understand why those who seemingly appear to have great abilities and strength are not putting them to good use. "Get on the road," they say, but the disciplined ones, those in God's harness, know better than to move before they hear the voice of the Master. They will move in His time, with purpose and great responsibility.

And the Lord let me to know that there were many whom He had brought into training who had rebelled against the discipline, the chastising of the Father. They could not be trusted with the great responsibility of mature son ship, so He let them go back to their freedom, back to their religious activities and revelations and gifts. They are still His people, still feeding in His pastures, but He has set them aside from the great purposes for this end of the age. So they revel in their freedom, feeling that they were the Chosen Ones with the many streams of living water, not knowing that they have been set aside as unfit for His great work in this end of this age.

He showed me that through the chastising seems grievous for the time, and the discipline hard to endure, yet the result with all the glory of son ship is worth it all, and the glory to follow far exceeds the Suffering we endure. And though some may lose even their lives in this training, yet they will share alike in the glory of His eternal purposes. So faint not saints of God, for it is the Lord that doth bring thee into confinement, not thine enemy. It is for thy good, and for His glory, so endure all things with praises and thanksgiving that He hath counted thee worthy to share His glory! Fear thou not the whip in His hand, for it is not to punish thee, but to correct and train thee, that thou mightiest come into submission to His will, and be found in His likeness in that hour. Rejoice in your trials, in all your tribulations, and glory in His cross, and in the confining limitations of His harness, for He hath chosen thee and He hath taken upon Himself the responsibility of keeping you strong and well fed. So lean upon Him, and trust not in your own ability and your own understanding. So shalt you may be fed, and His hand shall be upon you, and His glory shall overshadow you and shall flow through you as it goes forth to cover the earth. Glory to God! Bless the Lord, He's wonderful! Let Him be Lord of your life, friends, complain not at that which He bringeth to pass in your life.

And so to those who are brought into absolute subjection to His will, there is no law. For they move in the Grace of God, led only by His Spirit where all things are lawful but not all things are expedient. This is a dangerous realm for the undisciplined, and many have perished in sin as they leaped over the fence without His harness and His bridle. Some have thought themselves as being completely harnessed and submissive to Him, only to find that in some avenue of their lives there dwelled rebellion and self-will. Let us wait before Him until He puts His noose around us and draws us to His place of training. And let us learn of the dealings of God and the moving of His Spirit until at last we feel His harness drop about us, and hear His voice guiding us. Then there is safety from the traps and pitfalls of sin, and then we shall abide in His House forever!

On Pure Love

(**1 John 3:1-3**) *"Behold what manner of love the Father has bestowed on us, that we should be called sons of God: Therefore the world knoweth us not, because it knew Him not. Beloved, now are the sons of God, and it doth not yet appear what we shall be: but we know that, when He shall appear, we shall be like Him; for we shall see Him as He is. And every man that hath this hope in Him purifieth himself, even as He is pure."*

(**Matthew 22:36-40**) *"Master, which is the great commandment in the law?' Jesus said to him, 'thou shall love the LORD thy God with all thy heart, with all your soul, and with all thy mind. This is the first and great commandment. And the second is like unto it, thou shalt love thy neighbor as thyself. On these two commandments hang all the Law and the Prophets.'"*

(**Proverbs 16:4**) *"The Lord hath made all things for Himself: yea, even the wicked for the day of evil."*

It says; everything belongs to Him, and He will never release His right to anything. Free and intelligent creatures are His as much as those which are otherwise. He refers every unintelligent thing totally and absolutely to Himself, and He desires that his intelligent creatures should voluntarily make the same disposition of themselves.

It is true that He desires our happiness, but that is neither the chief end (goal) of His work, nor an end to be compared with that of His glory. It is for his glory only that He wills our happiness; the latter is a subordinate consideration, which He refers to the final and essential end of His glory.

That we may enter into His designs in this respect, we must prefer God before ourselves, and endeavor to will our own happiness for His glory; in any other case, we invert the order of things. And we must not desire His glory on account of our own salvation, but, on the other hand, the desire for His glory should impel us to seek our own happiness as a thing which He has been pleased to make a part of His glory. It is true that all holy souls are not (yet) capable of exercising this explicit preference for God over themselves, but there must at least be an implicit preference; the former, which is more perfect (ideal), is reserved for those whom God has endowed with light and strength to prefer Him to themselves, to such a degree as to desire their own happiness simply because it adds to His glory.

Men have a great repugnance to this truth, and consider it to be a very hard saying, because they are lovers of self which comes from self-interest. They understand, in a general but superficial way, that they must love God more than all His creatures, but they have no conception of loving God more than themselves, and loving themselves only for Him. They can utter these great words without difficulty, because they do not enter into their meaning, but they shudder when it is explained to them, that God and His glory are to be preferred before ourselves and everything else to such a degree that we must love His glory more than our own happiness, and must refer the latter to the former, as a subordinate means to an end.

(**Matthew 16:25**) *"For whoever will save his life shall lose it: and whoever will lose his life for my sake will find it."*

And Paul summed up our purpose this way:

(**Romans 11:36**) *"For of Him, and through Him, and to Him, are all things: to whom be glory forever. Amen."*

3 A DIFFERENT FAITH THE ANTI-RELIGION

(**Amos 8:11-12**) *"Behold, the days come, saith the Lord GOD, that I will send a famine in the land, not a famine of bread, nor a thirst for water, but of hearing the words of the LORD: And they shall wander from sea to sea, and from the north even to the east, they shall run to and fro to seek the word of the LORD, and shall not find it."*

(**2 Timothy 4:3-4**) *"For the time will come when they will not endure sound doctrine; but after their own lusts shall they heap to themselves teachers, having itching ears; and they shall turn away their ears from the truth, and shall be turned unto fables."*

(**2 Thessalonians 2:3-4**) *"Let no man deceive you by any means: for that day shall not come, except there come a falling away first, and that man of sin be revealed, the son of perdition; Who opposeth and exalteth himself above all that is called God, or that is worshipped; so that he as God sitteth in the temple of God, shewing himself that he is God."*

A new gospel

François-Marie Arouet, better known as Voltaire, is credited with the famous saying about man creating God in his own image. He worded it this way: "If God has made us in his image, we have returned him the favor." Many variations of this quotation have been used by various authors over the years to communicate the idea that man has a natural predisposition—the Bible calls it sin—to think of himself as the center of the universe. It was pointed out to me in a sermon I heard in my early days of becoming a Christian that man employs two methods of making more of himself than he ought. The first is fairly obvious: man makes much of himself. But the second is less obvious and more difficult to deal with: man makes little of God.

While it should be quickly stated that what generally happens is something of a combination of these two methods, it is nevertheless a fact that man has a difficult time being truly honest and forthright with himself about his position in the hierarchy of life. Saint Augustine understood this point well and expressed it quite clearly in his Confessions as part of his answer to the question of where (and what) evil comes from. Man is a creature by definition; he is not autonomous. Man was created by the Creator and therefore is dependent upon the Creator in order to properly understand himself. Sin arises when man begins to determine reality for himself, rather than listening to the Words of the Creator. When God delivered Adam's death sentence in the Garden, He prefaced it with these words:

(**Genesis 3:17**) *"And to Adam he said, Because thou hast hearkened unto the voice thy wife, and have eaten from the tree, of which I commanded thee, saying, thou shall not eat of it: cursed is the ground for thy sake; in sorrow shalt thou eat of it all the days of thy life;"*

Adam elevated himself to the position of judge; choosing to listen to the voice of his wife, rather than to the voice of God.

In the New Testament, Paul picks up on this idea and warns his readers to not be deceived as was Eve (**2 Corinthians 11:3 and 1 Timothy 2:14**). Paul is warning the Corinthian church that they are too passive in their faith. He reveals to them that they are too permissive and too willing to listen to anyone who happens to come along and tell them something about Jesus. He is cautioning them about being easily misled—easily deceived— just as Eve was by the serpent. Paul is saying that the Corinthian's have a propensity to try and get along with everyone. They don't like making waves; they want everybody to have their own version of Jesus and retain their autonomy too. In other words, Paul accuses the Corinthians of being theologically spineless:

(**2 Corinthians 11:19-20**) *"For ye suffer fools gladly, seeing ye yours selves are wise. For ye suffer, is a man bring you into bondage, if a man devour you, if a man take of you, if a man exalt himself, if a man smite you on the face."*

Unfortunately, much of modern evangelicalism has become like the Corinthians: unwilling to rock the boat of theological political-correctness so that everyone can find a seat in the all-inclusive, ecumenical ship of fools. It is this very situation of evangelical niceness and non-confrontation that is taking advantage of and using to smuggle his liberal political views into the church.

The identification of faith or positive thinking with success has been at the heart of the prosperity and health and wealth gospel movements among Pentecostal Christians. The prosperity gospel asserts that God wants believers to be healthy and wealthy in mind, body, and spirit. Prosperity results from our faith -- our willingness to believe, receive, and act upon God's promises of material and physical success. Alongside the Pentecostal prosperity gospel is the new thought or new age affirmation that people can create their own realities by visualization and positive thinking. Most recently, the best-selling new thought text, The Secret, affirmed that prosperity is solely the result of positive imaging and affirmative spirituality. If you get your thoughts right or have enough faith, these respective systems suggest that you will find wealth, health, and happiness.

Prosperity gospel

While there is much to affirm about the relationship of positive thinking, visualization, and heart-felt faith with physical, mental, relational, and spiritual well-being, I believe there are serious problems with both the new age/new thought and Pentecostal understandings of spirituality and prosperity. First, both are highly linear in approach: they assert that right thought or faith alone matters. If you have faith, you will succeed; if you don't, you will fail in every aspect of your life. Positive thinking ensures success; while negativity leads to disease and failure. Accordingly, both approaches neglect the relational and social nature of life. They believe that regardless of our environment, economic situation, physical condition, mental health, or family of origin, we will succeed if we only have enough faith or affirmative consciousness.

Second, both the prosperity gospel and new age optimism are highly individualistic: we succeed entirely as a result of our own faith or positive thinking and don't need the support of others; nor is it necessarily appropriate to interfere, especially in some new age versions, with the negativity that others experience. This viewpoint obviously has political and social consequences: there is a reason people are poor, and that reason is lack of faith or negative thinking. A less sophisticated understanding of poverty identifies the poor as lazy.

Third, both systems blame the victim for her or his failure: you don't get well because you lack faith or failure to plant a seed by a sufficient offering or because you harbor negative thoughts. Over the years, I have heard certain Christians lament, "if I only had enough faith, my child would get well." I have heard similar language for new thought/new age spiritual guides: your child is sick because of your negativity, or you are not recovering from cancer as a result of negative thinking. More than that, the authors of The Secret as well as new age luminary Louise Hay, clearly state that trauma, abuse, and accident are brought on by our negativity and that we choose to attract certain events in our lives.

I believe that Christians are called to affirm a new and more compassionate kind of prosperity gospel, one that affirms the life-transforming power of the faith and positive affirmations, but sees our affirmative faith in the context of many factors, including environment, economics, relationships, opportunity, etc. In contrast to linear causation, I assert that our well-being and suffering are the result of many interdependent factors, including God's lively vision for us and the impact of the social structure, and not just our own positive thinking, will, or faith. From a pastoral perspective, this is essential: we are not fully responsible for our success, ability to have faith, or current health condition. This encourages gratitude for the web of relationships that supports our success's as well as appropriate responsibility for our failures. The mind or faith are not omnipotent but always relational and contextual, and to some degree limited in power.

Second, while Christians are called to affirm the importance of a transformed mind, consciousness, or faith in well-being, we need to see personal transformation as emerging from and shaping the well-being of others. Our ability to have faith or hold positive images is not entirely our own doing -- poverty, sexism, ageism, homocentrism, etc., not to mention DNA, family of origin, or chemical balance -- can limit our ability to be optimistic.

Third, prosperity consciousness or faith is intended to contribute to the well-being of others. It has been stated that "God wants us to enjoy" and then followed with "God wants us all to enjoy." Those who believe in the power of the mind and faith to be factors in shaping body, mind, spirit, and relationship have the obligation to ensure that others have the basic environmental and relational foundations for that same well-being and success. While we are not entirely limited by our environment and can creatively transform negative scripts and experiences from childhood or the social order, ethical responsibility requires us to provide positive environments. Responsible positive thinking challenges us to create environments that are conducive to creativity, optimism, trust, and responsibility.

An authentic prosperity gospel encourages social responsibility and the creation of a social order that enables children and adults to dream dreams and cast visions and then have the social and relational resources to bring them to life.

Of course, to me, there's also a flips side. I think that this process involves a bit of soul searching and considering what it really means for us to be prosperous and successful. To me, prosperity and success isn't about the rush to acquire wealth and luxuries (though I admit that I do enjoy being financially comfortable and having a good number of luxuries), but about having a meaningful and pleasant life. And for me, that means having loved ones to share and celebrate my life with and to take part in their lives. I suppose this is why I often joke that there's no point in having a lot of money if I don't have people to spend it on.

I take my understanding of God from Jesus of course. He warned of the ultimate futility of the rush to acquire wealth. But he also confronted poverty and sickness as problems to be overcome. Thus, neither poverty or wealth were ideals for him, he sought to transcend both. I like his emphasis of giving over getting. One must have something to give in order to give, and one must hold it lightly in order to give.

The New Powerless Gospel

I have been challenged lately to think again about what the Gospel message is all about. This has come as a result of hearing what I consider to be, at the very least, "gospel lite" and at the most no gospel at all being presented by a number of neo-evangelicals, Third Wavers and outright heretics. The interesting thing is that many seem to be preaching the same message. What is most intriguing is that false teachers and ecumenical's, and even some preachers I would consider to be orthodox in their theology are preaching a "gospel" that is very similar.

The question is: Is this new gospel message really the Gospel at all?

The following is an example only. I am not stating that everyone is preaching this exclusively without mention of the cross, repentance, etc. But the new gospel goes something like this, with variations: "God loves you and has a plan for your life. He cares about you and wants to be a part of your life. You need to give in to Him and realize He has forgiven you for all the mistakes of your past, present and future. He wants you to be His child and wants to bless you with everything. Just come forward, decide for Jesus and ask Him into your heart."

Now, on the face of it, many people would have no problem with this presentation. Parts of the above are true. God is love. He can and does forgive. He wants us to be His children. God does bless those who belong to Him, although that is certainly not the whole story.

A major advantage of this new gospel is that it can be accepted by almost anyone of any religion. Read the above again and imagine yourself to be a New Ager, a Mormon, Hindu, and ect... Would it offend you to know that God loves you? Who would not want to have a relationship with a God who loves them? Who would not want to be blessed?

The trouble is this new gospel says nothing about repentance, recognition of guilt and the penalty of death for sins, or any true explanation of the sacrifice of Jesus Christ on the cross. This is clearly why those who preach this gospel are seeing so many profess faith in it.

Millions worldwide are able to accept this gospel without it interfering with their life in any significant way. There is no challenge presented that would cause anyone to have their world view completely changed, let alone their life.

This new gospel allows people to continue to do what they want and to be who they want to be. It's so easy. All they need to realize is that "God" loves them as they are. A small problem with this scenario is: who knows what "god" they have in mind when they place their belief in this new gospel message?

Although the above snippet of this modern "gospel-lite" does have some major flaws that I will get into in a moment, what is most conspicuous is what is NOT being presented.

The Missing Gospel ABCs, First of all, every presentation of the Good News should always have, what has been referred to by Josh McDowell as, the ABCs of the Gospel:

A - Admit you are a sinner: (**Romans 3:23, 6:23**)
B - Believe in the Gospel facts: (**1 Corinthians 15:1-8**)
  1. Jesus died to pay for your sin: (**Romans 5:6-8**)
  2. Jesus rose from the dead to show that the payment was accepted: (**2 Corinthians 5:21; Romans 6:4-5**)
C- Commit yourself to trusting in God's provision. Personally receive the gift: (**Romans 10:9-10**)

Every Gospel message should include these ABC's. These would necessarily include an explanation about the sin in every man that ends in death, the Atonement provided by Christ's death on the cross, the washing of the Blood of Christ shed for us because without blood being shed there is no forgiveness of sins, and the fact that when we believe we pick up our Cross and follow Christ to death also.

(**1 Corinthians 2:1-2**) *"And I, brethren, when I came to you, came not with excellency of speech or of wisdom, declaring unto you the testimony of God. For I determined not to know anything among you, save Jesus Christ, and him crucified."*

(**Galatians 6:14**) *"But God forbid that I should glory, save in the cross of our Lord Jesus Christ, by whom the world is crucified unto me, and I into the world."*

Paul preached the cross. Should we do any less?

Just Decide For Jesus

Another problem: What is all this "come to Jesus" or "decide for Jesus" stuff? These kind of statements gloss over the truth of the Gospel to the extent that it can no longer be properly understood by the non-believer, here is what we must understand.

Salvation comes not by "accepting the finished work" or "deciding for Christ". It comes by believing on the Lord Jesus Christ, the whole, living, victorious Lord who, as God and man, fought our fight and won it, accepted our debt as His own and paid it, took our sins and died under them and rose again to set us free. This is the true Christ, and nothing less will do. But something less is among us, nevertheless, and we do well to identify it so that we may repudiate it. That something is a poetic fiction, a product of the romantic imagination and maudlin religious fancy. It is a Jesus, gentle, dreamy, shy, sweet, almost effeminate and marvelously adaptable to whatever society He may find Himself in. He is cooed over by women disappointed in love, patronized by pro tem celebrities and recommended by psychiatrists as a model of a well integrated personality. He is never acknowledged as Lord. These quasi Christians follow a quasi Christ. They want His help but not His interference. They will flatter Him but never obey Him.

No Original Sin

Another flaw in this modern gospel presentation is the implication that man is not totally fallen but is partly good -- good enough for God to overlook the sinful parts -- good enough to aspire to have a relationship with God on our own merits -- in fact, good enough in the end to even aspire to godhood according to Third Wave heretics. This is all Pelegianism to the core. The new gospel is very much tied to a Pelegian concept of original sin, which is that there was no original sin that affected all mankind. It is implied that God loves our sinful part because He sees the good part in us. It is implied if not directly stated by some that there was no total fall in Eden but rather a broken relationship where God is just waiting for us to muster up enough "good" intentions and godly sorrow to come back to God who doesn't really care if we have sinned in the past, present or future.

To me this type of gospel nullifies the need for Christ's sacrifice on the cross. The Pelegians are wrong because the Bible says we are desperately wicked without cure.

(**Jeremiah 17:9**) *"The heart is deceitful above all things, and desperately wicked: who can know it?"*

(**Romans 3:10-12**) *"As it is written, There is none righteous, no, not one: There is none that understandeth, there is none that seeketh after God. They are all gone out of* *the way, they are together become unprofitable; there is none that doeth good, no not one."*

Only through the substitutionary sacrifice of God's Son on the cross can we be made righteous in the Father's eyes.

(**Romans 5:19**) *"For as by one man's disobedience many were made sinners, so by the obedience of the one shall many be made righteous."*

(**2 Corinthians 5:21**) *"For he hath made him to be sin for us, who knew no sin; that we might be made the righteousness of God in him."*

No Need for Faith

Another major fault I hear often in the new gospel presentations is, interestingly enough (because it is from the opposite side of the theological divide), a hyper-Calvinist tenant. It claims that we are made regenerate before we believe. The end result of this teaching is the concept that since God already decided to love some and hate others and that faith is a gift from God that He decided to dole out to some individuals for His own purposes, there is no need to believe, to have faith. This misrepresentation of the gospel teaches that we simply need to sort of understand what God has done for us and it will be made so, despite any decision we make or do not make.

The fourth point of Calvinism states: "I" = IRRESISTIBLE GRACE

The Calvinists believed that the Lord possesses irresistible grace that cannot be obstructed. They taught that the free will of man is so far removed from salvation, that the elect are regenerated (made spiritually alive) by God even before expressing faith in Jesus Christ for salvation. If a totally depraved person wasn't made alive by the Holy Spirit, such a calling on God would be impossible.

Surely seeing the kingdom of God is the act of faith and, if so, such faith is impossible without regeneration. Hence regeneration must be prior to faith. We can affirm then on these grounds that the order is regeneration, faith, justification. All we need is one verse to refute this false doctrine.

(**Ephesians 1:13**) *"In whom ye also trusted, after that ye heard the word of truth, the gospel of your salvation: in whom also after that ye believed, ye were sealed with that Holy Spirit of promise,"*

Notice that the Holy Spirit seals the believer the moment they believe, not before. We hear the gospel, we are convicted by the Holy Spirit, and we respond in faith, we believe, we are marked with the Holy Spirit. That is the biblical truth of the matter. But hyper-Calvinists go further: "A believer may come to the place of not believing, and yet God will not disown him, since He cannot disown Himself. This can also be disproved with a few verses:

(**Revelation 21:8**) *"But the fearful, and unbelieving, and the abominable, and murderers, and whoremonger, and sorcerers, and idolaters and all liars, shall have their part in the lake which burneth with fire and brimstone: which is the second death."*

(**Romans 11:20**) *"Well; because of unbelief they were broken off, and thou standest by faith. Be not high-minded, but fear."*

If the Jews, the chosen people of God, could be broken off because of unbelief, Paul warns us that we as Gentiles can also.

Belief is absolutely crucial to be saved

(**Romans 10:9-10**) *"That if thou shalt confess with thy mouth the Lord Jesus, and shalt believe in thine heart that God hath raised him from the dead, thou shalt be saved. For with the heart man believeth unto righteousness; and with the mouth confession is made unto salvation."*

(**Romans 3:22**) *"Even the righteousness of God which is by faith of Jesus Christ unto all and upon all them that believe: for there is no difference:"*

(**1Timothy 1:16**) *"Howbeit for this cause I obtained mercy, that in me first Jesus Christ might shew forth all longsuffering, for a pattern to them which should hereafter believe on him to life everlasting."*

Faith is an act of the will

I also do not believe that (**Ephesians 2:8-9**) is talking about faith being a gift from God, but rather it is referring to grace being that gift. This is confirmed by other passages that deal with the subject of the gift of grace such as (**Romans 5:15-17**). We never see the "gift of faith" mentioned in the Bible but instead (**Ephesians 2:8-9**) says "through faith" not as a result of God giving us our faith. (**Romans 11:6**) is not juxtaposing faith vs. works, but rather grace is shown to be the way to salvation and not works. So (**Ephesians 2:8-9**) is the same theme, the main topic being grace vs. works. The appropriation of that grace comes "through faith" alone. God does build us up in our faith, of which Jesus is the author (leader, pioneer, prince leader) if we choose to continue in faith.

(**Hebrews 12:2**) *"Looking unto Jesus the author and finisher of our faith; who for the* *joy that was set before him endured the cross, despising the shame, and is set down at the hand of the throne of God."*

With (**Hebrews 12:2**) we must keep in mind and we must also weigh the following:

(**Colossians 1:22-23**) *"In the body of his flesh through death, to present you holy and un-blamable and un-reprove able in his sight: If ye continue in the faith grounded and settled, and be not moved away from the hope of the gospel, which ye have heard, and which was preached to every creature which is under heaven; whereof I Paul am made a minister,"*

If that is the case, it would nullify the apostles many other teachings on the subject of holding, standing in, persevering, and overcoming by faith. In fact all those teachings become inane and useless, which is why you will hear very little teaching from hyper-Calvinists on the subject of holding on to faith (with regards to salvation), and nothing about the possible destruction of faith. Suffice it to say that God will build us up in our most holy faith if we submit to Him. However, God will never circumvent our free will to save us. Interestingly the Bible also teaches us that we must also build ourselves up in the Faith.

(**Jude 1:20**) *"But ye, beloved, building up yourselves on your most holy faith, praying in the Holy Ghost,"*

This is because faith is an act of the will, a very human decision made using our God-created will whereby we can decide to submit to the will of God and place all our hope of salvation in the grace of Jesus Christ alone. As God builds our faith, our faith grows. If we shrink back, our faith may be destroyed.

(**Hebrews 10:38-39**) *"Now the just shall live by faith: but if any man drawback, my soul shall have no pleasure in him. But we are not of them who draw back unto perdition; but of them that believe to the saving of the soul."*

(**Hebrews 11:1**) *"Now faith is the substance of things hoped for, the evidence of things not seen."*

The writer of Hebrews is talking about "my righteous one". "He" - the righteous one, can shrink back, but those who believe are saved. Apparently there were whose who had lost their faith in the Lord during the time Hebrews was written, but he is commending those he is writing to that they "are not of those who shrink back and are destroyed". Faith is holding on to the hope we have in the grace of Jesus Christ. God helps us hold on and strengthens that holding, but God's people can resist the Holy Spirit see (**Acts 7:51**), grieve Him see (**Ephesians 4:30**) shrink back see (**Hebrews 10:39**) shipwreck their faith see (**1 Timothy 1:19**) and fall away see (**2 Peter 1:10; Mark 4:17**). I won't debate with you as to the end of any person who shrinks back because the Holy Spirit continues to convict until such a time as is appointed by the Father.

My point is that faith is a two-way street. Jesus is the leader and will preserve our faith as we continue to hold on. I don't know how it works but I have to take Scripture at face value on this apparent antinomy. But I'm glad the Lord gives me a choice, aren't you?

The hyper-Calvinists, and those who incorporate this extreme Calvinist doctrine into the modern gospel message, are wrong because the Bible states over and over again that we cannot be saved without faith/belief.

(**Hebrews 11:6**) *"But without faith it is impossible to please him: for he that cometh to god must believe that he is, and that he is a rewarder of them that diligently seek him."*

(**Acts 16:31**) *"And they said, Believe in the Lord Jesus Christ, and thou shalt be saved, and thy house."*

(**Romans 10:9**) *"That if thou shalt confess with thy mouth the Lord Jesus, and shalt believe in thine heart that God hath raised him from the dead, thou shalt be saved."*

Faith is a freewill decision to place our hope in Christ in response to the conviction of the Holy Spirit and the work of the Spirit in the mind of the believer to help him come to faith in Christ.

(**Hebrews 11:1**) *"Now faith is the substance of things hoped for, the evidence of things not seen."*

(**John 16:8-11**) *"And when he is come, he will reprove the world of sin, and of righteousness, and of judgment: Of sin, because they believe not on me; Of righteousness, because I go to my Father, and ye see me no more; Of judgment, because the prince of this world is judged."*

We can see three elements in (**John 16:8-11**) that they are tied to the conviction of the Holy Spirit. These are also essential for inclusion in a gospel presentation:

(1) The problem of sin.
(2) The righteousness of Christ.
(3) And the judgment.

To summarize, I believe that because of teachings like this many are either never able to come to a true belief in Christ or that some are not continuing in their faith because they are placing their hope in another "Jesus", like the one who is at their beck and call for signs, wonders, miracles, and money. Suffice it to say that God will build us up in our most holy faith if we obey Him and submit to His will. However, God will never circumvent our free will to save us against our will. Lest we give God credit for something He urges us to decide to do, the Bible teaches us that we must build ourselves up in the Faith. This is a wonderful antinomy of both a free will decision on our part to build up our faith aided by the Holy Spirit, without Whom we would not even know how to pray see (**Romans 8:26**).

Faith is an act of the will, a very human decision within a God-created will to submit to the will of God with the conviction and help of the Holy Spirit, without whom we would never be able to come to faith in God. Jesus, the God/man, in His humanity made the same kind of free will decision to submit to the Father and lay down His will and finally His life for us on the cross. With the decision to believe we place all our hope of salvation in the grace of Jesus Christ alone. God created in us a conscience that is further aided by the Holy Spirit and made to comprehend the meaning of the salvation message when truly presented. The Spirit is able to convict the righteous and unrighteous alike. I believe we are also able to resist the conviction of the Holy Spirit to bring us to salvation and end up falling away, shipwrecking our faith.

No Penalty, No Repentance

Yet another problem with this modern defective gospel is to bring people to a belief in a God who is all love without His holiness causing Him to require the penalty of death for sin be paid by His only Son.

(**Romans 6:23**) *"For the wages of sin is death, but the gift of God is eternal life in Christ Jesus our Lord."*

This omission of the death penalty for sin nullifies the very need for a Savior and causes many to believe in a different god who is apparently willing to write off the death of his only son. The wages of sin is death. Without repentance we are doomed:

(**2 Peter 3:9**) *"The Lord is not slack concerning his promise, as some men count slackness; but is longsuffering to us-ward, not willing that any should perish, but that all should come to repentance."*

(**2 Corinthians 7:10**) *"For godly sorrow worketh repentance to salvation not to be repented of: but the sorrow of the world worketh death."*

(**Acts 3:19**) *"Repent ye therefore, and be converted, that your sins may be blotted out, then the times of refreshing shall come from the presence of the Lord,"*

It is not repentance that saves. Jesus Christ saves. But repentance is the only way to come to the point where a person sees his desperate condition and fully realizes his need for the Savior. Conviction of sin is a work of the Holy Spirit in concert with a will brought into submission to God. These concepts are what are almost totally absent from the modern gospel.

No Explanation

There are many other problems with this new gospel. I see an almost total lack of explanation about how and why the physical death of Jesus Christ on the cross is the only sacrifice for our sin.

(**Hebrews 10:10**) *"By the which will we are sanctified through the offering of the body of Jesus Christ once for all."*

There is almost no teaching on why Jesus had to die or the significance of His resurrection.

(**1 Peter 3:18**) *"For Christ also hath once suffered for sins, the just for the unjust, that he might bring us to God, being put to death in the flesh, but quickened by the Spirit."*

(**Romans 6:5**) *"For if we have been planted together in the likeness of his death, we shall be also in the likeness of his resurrection."*

There also seems to be a strong emphasis on the fact that we are accepted already by the Lord in our sinful condition and that we just need to allow Him to love us and bless us. I actually heard it preached that God loves the wicked. This is a wrong way of presenting the Gospel. God loves the creatures He created in the sense that He wants them to repent and turn to Him, placing their faith and trust in Jesus Christ alone for salvation. But He does not love wickedness or those who practice it. They must be saved or forever damned to hell in eternity.

(**Proverbs 8:13**) *"The fear of the LORD is to hate evil; pride, and arrogancy, and the evil way, and the forward mouth, do I hate."*

(**Psalms 97:10**) *"Ye that love the LORD, hate evil: he preserveth the souls of his* *saints; he delivereth them out of the hand of the wicked."*

(**Romans 12:9**) *"Let love be without dissimulation. Abhor that which is evil; cleave to that which is good."*

(**Luke 13:27**) *"But he shall say, I tell you, I know you not whence ye are; depart from me, all ye workers of iniquity."*

Finally, this kind of false gospel often leads into teachings on prosperity and confession, which is why it seems to be no problem for heretics to preach it.

A New Kind of Covenant

God's people had a covenant with God—an agreement that specified the conditions of their relationship. The terms laid out in the Book of Deuteronomy are reflected in:

(**Joshua 1:7**) *"Only be thou strong and very courageous, that thou mayest observe to do according to all the law, which Moses my servant commanded thee: turn not from it to be right hand or to the left, that thou mayest prosper whithersoever thou goest."*

When Achan sinned, God turned away from the Israelites. So when they battled the men of Ai, they were defeated. Thirty-six Israelites died. Joshua and the Israelites stoned Achan and his family and buried them beneath a large pile of stones as God commanded. These memorial stones reminded the people what we read in (**Romans 6:23**) *"For the wages of sin is death;"*

In the Bible story "The Defeat of Ai" from Joshua 8, God gave the Israelites another chance. He helped them ambush and destroy Ai—except this time God allowed them to plunder the city, keeping goods and livestock for themselves.

After their victory, Joshua built an altar to the Lord. He made burnt offerings and sacrificed peace offerings. Joshua wrote the law on stones. He read the book of the law to the people and renewed their covenant with the Lord.

God's presence with Israel was tied directly to their obedience to Him. Obedience led to blessing, and disobedience led to curses. See (**Deuteronomy 28**) Jesus came and fulfilled the old covenant. He initiated a new covenant, and the law is written now not on stones, but on our hearts and in our minds. See (**Jeremiah 31:33; Hebrews 10:16**)

As we teach we should, emphasize that when we repent and trust in Jesus, our right standing with God doesn't come from our obedience. It is not fazed by our disobedience.

While we may believe this with our minds, it is a difficult truth to trust with our hearts because it is so contrary to the way the world works, the way religion works.

Our salvation does not depend on our own works, but on Christ's finished work. He took the punishment we deserve, and His obedience brings our righteousness. (**Romans 5:19**) By faith in Jesus, we have victory over sin and death (**1 Corinthians 15:57**) and fellowship with God forever.

If Christianity is to receive rejuvenation, it must be by other means than any now being used. If the Church in the second half of this century is to recover from the injuries she suffered in the first half, there must appear a new type of preacher. The proper, ruler-of-the-synagogue type will never do. Neither will the priestly type of man who carries out his duties, takes his pay and asks no questions, nor the smooth-talking pastoral type who knows how to make the Christian religion acceptable to everyone. All these have been tried and found wanting.

Another kind of religious leader must arise among us. He must be of the old prophet type, a man who has seen visions of God and has heard a voice from the Throne. When he comes (and I pray God there will be not one but many), he will stand in flat contradiction to everything our smirking, smooth civilization holds dear. He will contradict, denounce and protest in the name of God and will earn the hatred and opposition of a large segment of Christendom. Such a man is likely to be lean, rugged, blunt- spoken and a little bit angry with the world. He will love Christ and the souls of men to the point of willingness to die for the glory of the One and the salvation of the other. But he will fear nothing that breathes with mortal breath.

Conclusion

I believe many are being inoculated against ever coming to true faith in Christ because of this "gospel" that is NOT the power unto salvation for those that believe in it. It only talks about the love of God and little or nothing about fearing the wrath of God, sin, repentance, or the cross of Christ. Without those things this new gospel is nothing but dust in the wind and doesn't have the power to save anyone.

4 APOSTASY IN THE CHRISTIAN CHURCH

(**2 Thessalonians 2:3**) *"Let no man deceive you by any means: for* that day shall not come, *except there come a falling away first, and that man of sin be revealed, the son of perdition;"*

As we have seen apostasy means to fall away from the truth. Therefore, an apostate is someone who has once believed and then rejected the truth of God. Apostasy is a rebellion against God because it is a rebellion against truth. In the Old Testament God warned the Jewish people about their idolatry and their lack of trust in Him. In the New Testament the epistles warn us about not falling away from the truth. Apostasy is a very real and dangerous threat in today's Church.

The verse at the top of the page tells us that there will be an apostasy that is associated with the appearance of the Antichrist. Most Christians are looking for the arrival of the Antichrist, but very few are looking for "the apostasy" that must come first. The arrival of the Antichrist cannot occur until sufficient apostasy has happened in the world. The Antichrist, who is the ultimate liar, cannot abide in a world where the truth of God's word is taught. This is why the Bible says that the apostasy will come first, and then the Antichrist will be revealed.

Therefore, we must, as Christians, ask this question "Is there an apostasy occurring in the Christian church today?" Some would say no and others yes. But, as we look for the arrival of the Antichrist, should we not also be looking for the arrival of apostasy? And where else should we first look but in our own house, for the Bible tells us that judgment will begin in the house of the Lord.

(**1 Peter 4:17**) *"For the time is come that judgment must begin at the house of God: and if it first begin at us, what shall the end be of them that obey not the gospel of God?"*

If there is indeed an apostasy occurring in the Christian Church, we would not know it unless we first examined the Bible closely and then compared the present-day Church to the Word of God. It is only after a standard of truth is established that we would then have a measuring rod by which apostasy can be detected. Therefore, I propose the following list of biblical truths as a sample of essential Christian and non-essential doctrines by which we might compare other teachings and phenomena. Note this is not absolute, and the nuances of several topics can be debated since not all will agree with the categorization of all points. Still, we need to use the Bible as our standard, and it gives us plenty of information by which we can know what the truth really is.

Primary Essentials (Nature and work of Christ)--Cannot deny and be Christian since they are explicitly stated as required in scripture.

- Jesus is both God and man (**John 1:1, 14; 8:24; Colossians 2:9; 1 John 4:1-4**)
- Jesus rose from the dead physically (**John 2:19-21**)
- Salvation is by grace through faith (**Romans 5:1; Ephesians 2:8-9; Galatians 5:1-5**)
- The gospel is the death, burial, and resurrection of Jesus (**1 Corinthians 15:1-4; Galatians 1:8-9**)
- There is only one God (**Exodus 20:1-3; Isaiah 43:10; 44:6, 8**)

Secondary Essentials--(Nature of God) you cannot deny and be Christian.

- God exists as a Trinity of persons: Father, Son, and Holy Spirit.
- Virgin Birth of Jesus--relates to incarnation of Christ as God and man.

Primary Non-Essentials (Bible, Church ordinances, and practice)
Denial does not void salvation, yet principles are clearly taught in scripture.

- Denial suggests apostasy.
- Male eldership and pastorate (**1 Timothy 2:12-13; 3:15; Titus 1:5-7**)
- Fidelity in marriage in heterosexual relationships (**1 Corinthians 6:9**)
- The condemnation of homosexuality (**Romans 1:26-27**)
- Inerrancy of Scripture (**2 Timothy 3:16**)

Secondary Non-Essentials--does not affect one's salvation relationship with God. Debated within Christianity. Denial or acceptance does not suggest apostasy.

- Baptism for adults or infants
- Predestination, election, and free will
- Communion every week, monthly, or quarterly, etc.
- Saturday or Sunday Worship
- Worship with or without instruments, traditional or contemporary.
- Pre-tribulation rapture, mid-tribulation rapture, post-tribulation rapture.
- Pre millennialism, a millennialism, and post millennialism.
- Continuation or cessation of the charismatic gifts Etc.

Of course, the non-essentials are debatable (which unfortunately leads to denominational fragmentation). But by way of explanation, the Primary Essentials are those doctrines that the Bible states if they are denied, damnation follows. For brevity, the Bible states that if you deny Jesus is God, you are dead in your sins; (**John 8:24, 58 cf. Exodus 3:14**) that if you deny Jesus' physical resurrection, your faith is in vain; (**1 Corinthians 15:14, cf. John 2:19-21**) that if you add works to salvation, you are not in Christ; (**Galatians. 3:1-3; 5:1-4**) and that if you preach a gospel contrary to what the apostles preached, you are accursed. (**Galatians 1:8-9, cf., 1 Corinthians 15:1-4**) Therefore, to deny any of these doctrines, according to scripture, is to be outside the camp of Christ and invited eternal damnation. This would obviously be apostasy.

The Secondary Essentials are essentials that further clarify orthodoxy, but there is no explicitly scriptural statement regarding each (that I am aware of) which states that denying them results in damnation the way the Primary Essentials do. The Secondary Essentials deal with the nature of God--primarily. The fact that there is one God who is a Trinity is clearly essential to Christian orthodoxy, but there is no scriptural statement stating that to believe in the Trinity is necessary for salvation. However, that does not mean that denial of the Trinity is acceptable. A person can be saved without knowing about the Trinity. But, since the Trinity is a biblical truth and the believer is indwelt by the Holy Spirit who bears witness of truth, a true Christian will not openly denounce the Trinity once he has been taught it from scripture. So, it could be said that the Secondary Essentials are essentials to the faith as well as the Primary Essentials are.

The Primary Non-Essentials are biblical teachings that if denied do not affect one's salvation. But, because the Bible teaches them, denying them is a sign of apostasy. The Secondary Non-Essentials do not affect one's position with God, nor do they affirm or deny biblical teaching since they are debatable. Having differing beliefs in these is not a sign of apostasy--just differences of opinion. Again, I am aware that the categorization of the non-essentials is debatable, but I must draw the line somewhere. Sadly, it is in Secondary non-essential doctrines that most denominational fragmentation occurs. This is a sad display that most division occurs over that which is least important. Furthermore, I believe that it is in the area of the Non-Essentials that apostasy can first be detected.

(**2 Thessalonians 2**) *"That ye be not soon shaken in mind, or be troubled, neither by spirit, nor by word, nor by letter as from us, as that the day of Christ is at hand."*

As quoted above, there is a prophecy in 2 Thessalonians about a coming apostasy that is associated with the disclosure of the anti-Christ.

(**2 Thessalonians 2:3**) *"Let no man deceive you by any means: for that day shall not come, except there come a falling away first, and that man of sin be revealed, the son of perdition;"*

Have you been looking for the coming of the anti-Christ? Are you waiting for him to pop up on the world scene? If you are, are you also looking for the related apostasy? Most Christians are looking for the anti-Christ but are not looking for signs of apostasy.

The Bible is God's word, and it tells us what is right and wrong. To the degree that anyone disagrees with the truths of God's word, to that same degree they are falling away from it. What, then, might be some of the signs of apostasy? I've compiled a representative list of issues. You may or may not agree with all of these, but I provide them as food for thought.

1. Denial of basic Christian doctrines such as the Trinity, the deity of Christ, the deity of the Holy Spirit, salvation by grace, and moral absolutes as found in the Bible.
   a. God's word is true. Deviation from the basics of its truth is surely apostasy.
2. Countless denominational divisions that contradict. (**John 13:35 and 1 Corinthians 1:10**)
   a. Of course, there are bound to be divisions in the body of Christ; and differences of opinions are permitted. (**Romans 14:1-12**) But, the amount of divisions in the Church is ridiculous and contrary to (**Colossians 3:14**)
3. Ordination of homosexuals
   a. Homosexuality is clearly condemned in God's word. (**Leviticus 18:22; 1 Corinthians 6:9**) To ordain homosexuals

into ministry is clearly contrary to biblical truth and clearly apostasy.

4. Women elders and pastors
   a. Whether people like it or not in this politically correct environment, the Bible does not support women as elders or as pastors. (**1 Timothy 2:12-14; 3:2; Titus 1:5-7**) Men are called to be leaders in the church. The fact that women elders and pastors exist is a sign that men are not doing their God-given job.

      Also, if you believe in women pastors and elders, do not dismiss this article. You must always examine yourself to see if what you believe is biblical.

5. Not preaching the gospel per (**1 Corinthians 15:1-4**)
   a. The gospel is the death, burial, and resurrection of Jesus for our sins. It is not a message of convenience or embarrassment. Do not be ashamed of the gospel. (**Romans 1:16**)

6. Using the Lord's name in vain, something a surprising number of Christians does.
   a. God's name and title are to be used only by Christians in a reverent and respectful manner--never in casual exclamation. Just because the sinners do it, does not mean it is okay for the Christians.

7. Not sending out or failing to support missionaries (or cutting back unnecessarily) in violation of. (**Matthew 28:18-20**)
   a. Carrying out the Great Commission is the command of Jesus. Any church that is able to support missionary work and does not is in direct violation of Christ's command in the Great Commission.

8. Marketing and merchandising.
   a. Those in ministry should make a living from their labor. Churches should seek to spread the gospel best they can and selling things to do it is acceptable. But, how many trinkets and bobbles are offered in the name of Christ that do not honor God but are merely for the purpose of financial gain? Is the duty of the church business or the gospel? Remember how Jesus cleansed the temple?

9. Pastors who are more concerned with growing a church than preaching the truth.
   a. Whoever and wherever they are, they need to repent. Pastors must stand on the truth of God's word even if it costs them financially and materially.

10. Pastors who don't pray and seek God's face.

    a.   Of course, this should be rare. But, any pastor who does not seek God's face in humility is seeking to do a job--not a ministry--under his own power.

11. Pastors who cave in to pressures from the church in contradiction to the word of God.

    a.   Any pastor who does this should repent now or step down from the pulpit. Pastors are to stand upon and for God's word no matter what the obstacles or the cost.

12. Pastors who fail to equip their congregations according to God's word.

    a.   Pastors are called to equip the Christian for the work of the ministry in all aspects of life; (**Ephesians 4:11**) apologetics, evangelism, missionary work, prayer, service, love, etc. Far too many congregations are not being equipped with even the basics of Christianity and are instead being taught political correctness.

13. Pastors who don't teach damnation.

    a.   We are not saying that you must preach fire and brimstone all the time. But the fact is the gospel that offends no one is not the gospel of the Bible. The truth of the gospel is that people will face damnation. This is part of the Christian message, and it should be part of Christian preaching.

14. Christians gathering teachers to themselves to make them feel good.

    a.   Is comfort or truth the primary objective for the Christians? Are we divine in nature or sinners saved by grace? Do we deserve to be saved, or are we saved by God's free choice? Christians who want merely to be entertained and comforted from the pulpit are still children. They should be challenged to grow and take risks.

15. Evolution.

    a.   Denominations that either adopt evolutionary principles or refuse to take a stand on evolution.

Apostasy is all around us in varying degrees. As Christians, we need to be very sure that we are clinging to the truth of God's word and resisting the inclusion of liberalism, moral relativism, and the oncoming secularism that is all around us. We need to stand on the word of God and never be ashamed of the truth of the Gospel: "For I am not ashamed of the gospel, for it is the power of God for salvation to everyone who believes, to the Jew first and also to the Greek." (**Romans 1:16**)

SUMMARY:

This is a sad and pitiful state of affairs. But it is true. Jesus said, "*I am come in My Father's name, and ye receive me not: If another shall come in his own name, him ye will receive.*" (**John 5:43**)

Here is another clue as to how this apostasy or 'great falling away' (**2Thesalonians 2:3**) from the faith will happen. Jesus said these very telling words to His disciples and covenant people. He told us just what spiritual qualities we would be looking for in our ultimate leader in the last days. Apparently we will want a selfish strongman, yes, even a sort of "Fuhrer".

At a future point in history, at the threshold of a great and epic moment of decision a global power broker and peacemaker will emerge onto the scene. He will confirm a covenant or treaty with 'many' for an agreed on period of seven years. Will Israel and the unified established western Church sign themselves over to this man? This will be the burning question and the intro into the end-time drama. What will they do, sign on, or not to sign on?

5 THE MAN OF SIN

The age of the Antichrist

(**2 Thessalonians 2:3-4**) *"Let no man deceive you by any means: for that day shall not come, except there come a falling away first, and that man of sin be revealed. The son of perdition: Who opposeth and exalteth himself above all that is call God, or that is worshipped; so that he as God sitteth in the temple of God, showing himself that he is God."*

According to the bible, the antichrist is coming, cf. (**1 john 2:18**) the one who engineers the final onslaught of Satan against Christ and the saints sometime just prior to the time when our Lord Jesus Christ establishes his kingdom on earth. Paul's terms for the antichrist are the "man of sin" and "the son of perdition." (**2 Thessalonians 2:3**) Other terms used in the Bible are the "beast (rising) up out of the sea" (**Revelation 13:1-10**), "a scarlet colored beast" (**Revelation17:3**) and "the beast." cf. (**Revelation 17:8, 16; 19:19-20; 20:10**)

A sign of the antichrist's coming

Unlike the rapture, the coming of the antichrist will not be without warning. There are several signs that will point to his coming and his appearance. There are at least three events that must occur before he makes his appearance on earth:

1. The "mystery of iniquity:" This is already at work in the world, but it will intensify. (**2 Thessalonians 2:7**)

   The "mystery of iniquity," that behind-the-scenes activity of evil powers evident throughout the world, will increase until it reaches its climax in the complete ridicule of and disregard for any standards and commandments held sacred in the Bible.

2. The "falling away must come:" This is beginning to happen (**2 Thessalonians 2:3**)

    Because of a prevailing spirit of lawlessness, the love of many will grow cold (**Matthew 24:10-12;** cf. **Luke 18:8**). Yet a faithful remnant will remain loyal to the apostolic faith as revealed in the New Testament. (**Matthew 24:13; 25:10; Luke 18:7**) Though these faithful people, the church will remain a warrior church, wielding the sword of the Sprit until is taken out of the world. See (**Ephesians 6:11**)

    The "apostasy" that Paul talks about will occur in the last days, multitudes within the professing church will depart from Biblical truth.

3. "he who now letteth" (the church) The church must be removed (**2 Thessalonians 2:7**)

    The church will taken away with the rapture thus freeing the devil to have free ring.

Both the apostle Paul and Christ depict a dismal picture of the condition of much of the visible church-morally, spiritually, and doctrinally – as the present age closes. (**cf. Matthew 24:5, 10-13, 24; 1Timothy 4:1; 2 Timothy 4:3– 4**) Paul in particular stresses that the churches will be invaded by godless elements in the last days.

This "falling away" within the church will have two dimensions.

1. Theological apostasy: is the departure from and rejection of a part or all of the original teaching of Christ and the apostles. (**Timothy 4:1; 2 Timothy 4:3**) False leaders will offer salvation and cheap grace and ignore Christ's demand for repentance, and separation from immorality, and loyalty to God and His standards. (**Peter 2:1-3, 12-19**) False gospels centering on human desires, needs, and goals of self-interest will become more and more popular.

2. Moral apostasy: is the severing of one's saving relationship with Christ and returning to sin and immorality. Apostates may proclaim right doctrine and N.T. teaching, yet abandon God's moral standards. (**Isaiah 29:13; Matthew 23:25-28**) Many churches will tolerate almost anything for the sake of numbers, money, success, and honor. The gospel of the cross with its call to suffer reproach from the world, (**Philippians**

1:29) to radically renounce sin, (**Romans 8:13**) to sacrifice for the kingdom of God, and to deny one's self will become rare. (**Matthew 24:12; 2 Timothy 3:1-5; 4:3**)

Both the history of the church and the predicted apostasy of the last days warn all believers not to take for granted a continual progress of the kingdom of God though all ages until the end. At some point in time in the worldwide history of the church, rebellion against God and His Word will reach astounding proportions. The day of the Lord will bring God's wrath upon those who reject his truth. (**1 Thessalonians 5:2-9**)

The ultimate triumph of God's kingdom and His righteousness in the world, therefore, depends not in the gradual increase of the success of the professing church, but on the final intervention of God when He breaks into the world with righteous judgment.

A pivotal and decisive event must occur before the "man of sin" can be revealed and the day of the Lord and its tribulation begins, (**2 Thessalonians 2:3-3**) namely, the taking "out of the way" of someone (**2 Thessalonians 2:7**) or something that "letteth" the mystery of iniquity and the 'man of sin". (**2 Thessalonians 2:3-6**) "Letteth" is an old English word meaning "obstruct, hold back, restrain." Then he who holds back the man of sin is taken out of the way, and then the day of the Lord can begin. (**2 Thessalonians 2:6-7**)

"*He who now letteth* (restraineth)" (**2 Thessalonians 2:7**) may best be understood as referring to the Holy Spirit, who alone has the power to hold back iniquity, the man of sin, and Satan. (**2 Thessalonians 2:9**) The restrainer is referred to by both the masculine ("*he, who now letteth,*" (**2 Thessalonians 2:7**) and by the neuter ("*what whitholdeth,*" (**2 Thessalonians 2:7**) likewise, the word for "Spirit" in the Greek language can be referred to by a masculine or neuter pronoun.

At the beginning of the final seven years of tribulation, the Holy Spirit will be "taken out of the way". (**2 Thessalonians 2:7**) This does not mean He is taken out of the world, but only that His restraining influence against lawlessness and the antichrist's entrance will cease. All restraints against sin will be removed and the satanically inspired rebellion will begin. However, the Holy Spirit will remain on during the tribulation to convict people of their sins, convert them to Christ, and empower them. See (**Revelation 7:9, 14; 11:1-11; 14:6-7**)

The Holy Spirit being taken out of the way enables the man of sin to come on the scene. (**2 Thessalonians 2:3-4**) God will send a deluding influence upon all those who have refused to love the truth they will accept the claims of the man of sin, and human society will degenerate to a depth of depravity never seen before.

The Holy Spirit's sin-restraining ministry is carried on largely though the

55

church, which is the temple of the Holy Spirit. (**1 Corinthians 3:16; 6:19**) Therefore, many interpreters believe the Holy Spirit being taken out of the way is a strong indication that the rapture of the faithful will occur at the same time. (**1 Thessalonians 4:17**) That is, the return of Christ to gather the overcomers of His churches unto Himself and to deliver them from the coming wrath (**1 Thessalonians 1:10**) will occur before the beginning of the day of the Lord and at the time when the man of sin is revealed.

Some scholars believe that the restrainer of (**2 Thessalonians 2:6**) (neuter gender) refers to the Holy Spirit and His restraining ministry, while in (**2 Thessalonians 2:7**) the "*he who now letteth*" (masculine gender) refers to the believers who are gathered together to Christ and taken out of the way, i.e., ruptured to meet Christ in the air in order to be with the Lord. (**1 Thessalonians 4:17**)

Compromise

It seems that the crowds in Israel and in Christendom will apparently favor giving total power to a leader, even if he is steeped in evil and selfish ways. We are already seeing that to a degree. However, this end stage humanism/selfishness will climax with that "awful horror" midway through the 70th week. This "abomination of desolation" was spoken of by Jesus in (**Matthew 24**). Jesus confirmed what Daniel had prophesied in (**Daniel 9:27**). He said that the "abomination that makes desolate" will be seen standing in the holy place and that this will initiate the Great Tribulation. (**Matthew 24:15-21**)

Selfishness is the hallmark of both "secular humanism" and "religious humanism". The dark spirit will not just be a secular reality. It will come inside the church as well. (**Daniel 9:27**) Selfishness is even now a Trojan horse even now parked just outside the church. After the (**Daniel 9:27**) deal it will be trundled on into the church. The fact that "religious humanism" is unrecognized and not spoken of shows just how far we have been deceived. And it shows the extent of our present danger. The awful compromise of religious humanism inside the church will eventually debauch the faith altogether. This will inevitably lead on to the cessation of sacrifice and homage to God Almighty the Holy One of Israel. Homage and oblation to the God of our Lord and Saviour Jesus Christ will be replaced by homage to an abominable sacrilege, the 'abomination that makes desolate'.

So just how far has the Christian church gone into this mire of compromise and double dealing? The church is even now preparing to desert the "patriarchal" God of Abraham, Isaac and Jacob in favor of a more globally acceptable "generic god". The marriage and ordination of homosexuals along with the acceptance of infanticide/partial birth abortion are just some of the gross and heinous sins covered up and "normalized" inside the church. How many Christians are faithful to the God of the scriptures? And just how many in the church will sign on with this global megadeal? The answer is, we do not know. But we shall find out as the 70th week opens and the 7 year covenant is signed. The WCC and the United Religions Initiative have already begun to negotiate with the powers of this world. Many "roundtables" and "dialogues" are already in session. Many well meaning but dangerously seduced Christian leaders have been invited to attend and are 'going over' to 'have a look'. Religious peace in the world is the key to world peace we are told. "Tolerance", "inclusiveness" and "understanding" are the catchwords. A lot of money and religious prestige is spread out on the table. Great opportunities for politico-religious activity are being offered by these emerging global entities. All sorts of new religious positions, privileges and perks are up for grabs. Many think this is a good thing. World peace is worth giving up nearly everything, (or so they say). Some are even ready to sell their most precious faith down the river. To them holiness seems to be a matter of human "choice", - just like abortion, homosexuality and perhaps gargoyle selection and steeple height.

Compromise is an awful thing. This is well known to those who know the God of the Bible. Warnings from scripture about mixing "*the cup of Christ with the cup of devils*" (**1 Corinthians 10:21**) do not seem be a source of concern for those brazen church leaders who would dare to bring grief to the Judeo-Christian God who came in the flesh as Jesus Christ fully revealing the character of our God. But the scripture, brought to us by our dear faithful Daniel tells us the outcome of all this compromise. Three and a half years into this 7 year "covenant" this other "*prince who is to come*" will replace the true service of God with an unspeakable abomination. (**Matthew 24:15-21**) This prince, who has now been "revealed" as "the beast", along with the ten global rulers will double-cross the very same religious double dealers who compromised the cup of Christ and bent over backwards in order to accommodate him. (**Revelations 17:16-18**)

This deal of awful compromise spoken of in Daniel is the great apostasy. This is the issue initiating the crisis of the end times. This act of high treason against the King of Kings is what starts the drama of the final 7 years, namely, the much discussed '70th week of Daniel'.

Let us pause here and ask ourselves a question. Have there been watershed moments in past church history when the ecclesiastical powers of established Christianity have bought into grievous compromise with the world and its systems? There most certainly has been. The prototypical accommodation that the church made was back in 325 A.D... At that time the church was invited to "go up" to sit at covenant with the Roman Caesar Constantine. There is no question that the Council of Niece was a watershed moment in church history. The compromise with the worldly powers led western civilization into the Dark Ages for one thousand years.

After a millennium of darkness, Gutenberg's printing press and the work of Bible translators brought the first glimmers of the gospel light back into mainstream Europe.

This history is all very interesting and instructive for us. But this future accommodation by the church, this 7 year covenant with a world prince as laid out for us by the angel Gabriel in (**Daniel 9:27**) will be an even greater debacle. It will be a wrong turn in the pathway leading to grievous consequences for many. This covenant with 'many' will involve many of God's people. The deal these deceived ones are destined to make with the coming peacemaker will be a church-state, Israel-Internationalist mega-deal. It will be much bigger in scope than Niece and far worse in its implications.

Somewhere up ahead in our future church history and in the history of Judah and the nation of Israel, lies a crucial fork in the road. It will give the people who think that they belong to the God of Abraham, Isaac, and Jacob a choice. Two roads will be laid out before us in that epic future day. One road will lead through a strait gate of persecution, trials, and tribulation. The other is wide and easy, a popular broad way. The difficult road is the Paradise road. That road will lead on to glory. But the broad way is the road to perdition. That smooth and easy road will lead on to deeper compromise and eventual abandonment of the eternal covenant of YHVH/Christ/Messiah. That broad way that looked so 'nice' will be deceiving. It will lead the traveler onwards to apostasy. And at the judgment they will face eternal torment in the fires of hell.

So much for church deals with secular kings and princes. Can we learn from this earlier church folly? Pray God we shall, because the church will be asked to revisit Niece. It seems that the church state deal we have at present is not compromised enough for the emerging secular powers. Ah, yes. We shall be asked to "renegotiate" the Niece deal. Eventually the epic (**Daniel 9:27**) megadeal with a humanistic global power-broker will open the 70th week.

This event, my dear brothers and sisters, is of critical importance to be aware of. This covenant between God's people and the principalities and powers of darkness is the crucial starting gun for the 70th week of Daniel and the final 7 years of this age. This event is what initiates the end-time drama.

Now is the time for us to draw near to our God. He knows all about this coming apostasy. And He has made abundant provision for us by His divine grace and favor.

Here is what the Bible says. There will indeed be an apostasy. A look at the World Council of Churches and the United Religions Initiative shows that the established church is even now deep into this false covenant with the emerging New World Order. So rather than neglect these lessons as "negative" we had best pay attention. There are many examples of abandonment in scripture. One classic case of dereliction of duty is laid out for us in (**Acts 27**). This recounts the story of the shipwreck of the Apostle Paul. Let us look at them and learn. Then let us all seek the face of our God. He knows exactly where we are. And He always takes care of His own.

Having shared that basic truth let us go one step further.

Why do we not recognize dereliction and apostasy when we see it? Is it Disneyized western Laodicean religious folklore that just happens to sell well to the profane quasi-Christian crowds in the religious marketplace? And does this actually "cloak" the real story of the apostasy by "many" in the 70th week so we don't hear the warning trumpets sound forth on that epic future day when the prophesied deal spoken of in (**Daniel 9:27**) is signed?

Let us pause to take stock here. The Church, just like ancient Israel has a problem. The heart of that problem is the tricky Jacob character trait and playing fast and loose with the end-time fidelity to Jesus Christ. Pagans and sinners out there in the secular world are not the problem. But a compromised double dealing church certainly is. Nice and easy superficial religion built upon half truths and 'cover stories' crafted for the nominal Christian masses may make for a profitable religious-business. But the true saints arriving at this critical time in holy history deserve better than this. So these half-truths just won't 'cut it'.

Brothers and sisters in Christ we need the truth. We need the truth so that we can be motivated to seek the face of God and repent. We need to seek the oil of His anointing to prepare our hearts for the coming trials. Why? Because we are His witnesses! This judgment is not a terrible thing. It is merely an opportunity for a refining and separation of the gold from the dross.

All these "nice" spins on the scriptures negate the necessity for us to seek His Presence in our lives. Like the five wise virgins we are to prepare ahead of time. Darkness is coming. We are to procure the oil of the Holy Spirit for the lamps of our spirit against the coming night.

If the saints knew this information would we do things differently? Would we get up from the ballgame or the soap opera or the stock market report and seek the face of God? Perhaps we might. And this would be good. This disturbance to our comfort agenda which our flesh says is "negative" is actually exceedingly "positive". And as for future trials we need not worry about them if we have committed ourselves to God and our lives to His witness. If certain "adventures" in future times do take us away from the cares of this world and on into God where we belong then this will turn out to be a redemptive serendipity for us. Could tribulation actually be the "good grief" that Charlie Brown in the 'Peanuts' comic strip always knew was coming and always agonized about? If so, what is so 'good' about it?

We shall find out.

Pray God that in the times to come we are found as faithful servants of the King. I realize this has been a heavy dissertation, but I beg of you all to stay with me here. These words of caution are not sent to scatter, but to restore the saints to their true and glorious destiny. They are sent, not to dismember, but rather to cause the saints to remember the eternal covenant. This has been secured for us by the shed blood of the promised Sacrifice of the Lamb. He is the Redeemer of Israel, Yeshua Hamashiach and our Lord Jesus Christ. He is outside, knocking at the door of our heart. Shall we let Him come in?

In the Jewish marriage betrothal the Bridegroom sets the cup before the prospective bride. She either drinks the cup in total commitment to her Betrothed, or she walks out on him. The new covenant is the cup and blood of Christ and is in like manner set before us.

The coming man of Sin

The coming global peacemaker, who is probably even now working behind the scenes, will ask us to go even further into pagan admixture. To participate, to profit, to even be licensed to operate legally, the church denominations will be asked to mix the cup of Christ with all the other religions of the world. This concession will be called for in the interests of "unity" it will be all inclusive and will offer world peace. This end-time renegotiating of the Nicene accord in politics and religion to embrace not just Christianity but also Buddhism, Islam, Wicca, and animism and the deadly Lucifer selfishness is what really starts the 7 year drama, NOT the rapture. This is the hidden church compromise that attempts to cover up the reality of the end time witness.

A battle royal is raging in the church even among evangelicals and charismatic's right now over this telling scripture given to us in (**Daniel 9:27**). The rejecting and twisting of the message in (**Daniel 9:27**) by the Kingdom Now or Dominion Theology movement is alarming. Furthermore we are seeing a resurgence of preterism and partial preterism. Partial preterism is more subtle and sinister version of preterism. If they cannot feed a full lie to the saints they will try a half lie. It is a cover job, a "cloaking" of the real truth. It is instigated by lesser angelic rulers in the lower heavens who rule over those who do not recognize the Lordship of Jesus Christ or the authority of the Holy Scriptures. These angelic powers preside over nations, religions, marketplaces and over the religious hirelings operating on their behalf.

The antichrist's activities

As the day of the Lord begins, the "man of sin" is revealed. He will be a world ruler who will make a covenant with Israel seven years before the end of the age. See (**Daniel 9:27**)

His true identification will be confirmed three and one-half years later as he breaks his covenant with Israel, becomes the world ruler, declares himself to be God, desecrates the temple in Jerusalem and forbids the worship of the Lord, and devastates the Land of Palestine.

The antichrist will declare himself to be God and will severely persecute those who remain loyal to God and Christ. He will demand worship, evidently form the temple that he uses as the canter of his pronouncements. Humans have sought this status since the beginning of creation.

The "man of sin" will demonstrate though the power of Satan great signs, wonders, and miracles in order to propagate error. (**2 Thessalonians2:9**) "Lying wonders" means that they are genuine supernatural miracles that deceive people into accepting a lie. It is possible these demonstrations of the supernatural will be seen on television around the world. Millions will be impressed, deceived, and persuaded by this highly persuasive and popular leader because they have no deep commitment to or love for the truth of God's Words. (**2 Thessalonians 2:9-12**)

Both (**2 Thessalonians 2:9**) and (**Matthew 24:24**) should caution believers to not assume that everything that is miraculous comes from God. Apparent "manifestations of the Spirit" (**1 Corinthians 12:7-10**) and alleged experiences from god of the Holy Spirit must be tested by the person's loyalty to Christ and Scripture.

The defeat of the antichrist

At the end of the tribulation, Satan will gather together many nations at Armageddon under the direction of the antichrist and make war against God and His people in a battle that will involve the entire world. When that occurs, Christ will return and supernaturally intervene to destroy the antichrist, his armies, and all who do not obey the gospel. Thereupon Christ will bind Satan and establish His kingdom in earth. (**Revelation 20:1-6**)

The prophet Daniel indicates that God's covenant people in Israel and in the Church will go along with this prince. (**Daniel 9:27**) So did Moses in the Song of Moses. So did Jesus Himself. (**John 5:43**)

This coming peacemaker, whom Daniel calls "*And after threescore and two weeks shall Messiah be cut off, but not for himself: and the people of the prince that shall come shall destroy the city and the sanctuary; and the end thereof shall be with a flood, and unto the end of the war desolations are determined.*" (**Daniel 9:26**) will confirm a 7 year covenant involving the sovereignty of Israel and the western nations. This will be a confirmation of a covenant that was previously in the works but unable to be consummated. Is it the end event of the present day "Road Map to Peace in the Middle East"? The Bible clearly tells us that events will come to pass that change the present political landscape. This man will open up a deal with God's people that will draw many of them on to the ultimate abomination that makes desolate at the midpoint of the 70th week. After this initial deal the world will never be the same. The trumpets will blow and this world will be on its way into the final seven years of this age.

This humanistic 7 year covenant will certainly be an unprecedented compromise in which Israel will give their holy land away. The west will hand their national sovereignty away to a global megadealer. There will be consequences to this. This man will be a selfish Lucifer an. He will lead many of God's covenant people on to deeper apostasy and to an abandonment of YHVH/Jesus Christ in the prophesied Great Falling Away of. (**2Thessalonians 2**)

Daniel tells us the story in that crucial verse of. (**Daniel 9:27**) Half way through those 7 years the future world ruler, the false messiah, will be possessed by the most abominable beast demon this world has seen since the days of Antiochus Epiphanes. He will break the covenant he made with Israel and stop the Temple sacrifices. He will then set up the "*abomination that makes desolate*" which both Daniel and Jesus spoke of. He will then be "revealed" as "the beast". At that time he will be supreme dictator of the world. And there is no surprise as to what happens next. The beast-man will turn around and demand total commitment to him.

Midway through the last 7 years of this age the Beast-Antichrist will establish his 666 economic systems. This will be a worship based on some sort of blood covenant marking of citizens. This will be the ultimate apostasy. That 666 blood covenant marking, whatever it turns out to be, will be a sign before men, angels, and God of their eternal allegiance to him. It may involve an ID mark, a tattoo, or an implantable chip. With this blood covenant initiation they bring their witness and show their devotion to the Beast.

Is the church prepared to witness in the face of this? How devoted is the average Christian believer in the west today? How likely is it that many will slip off into apostasy?

Many faithful Christians will make their stand in witness in those future days just as they are doing in China and in the Islamic world today. They will give their lives in martyrdom just as they have done in times past. But then God will also provide a Way of escape for His people just as He did before in the former exodus. Will many saints go off into exile at Bozrah? Apparently so, Jesus will return as the Deliverer not only at Jerusalem but also at a place called Bozrah.

There is some intriguing evidence of this exile in Revelation 12 where the woman in travail is given the wings of a great eagle and taken to a place where she can be nurtured for 1260 days as seen in (**Revelation 12:6**). This is also 3.5 biblical years. (**Revelation 12:14**) See both scriptures here have the very same time span, 42 biblical months, is given by John for both the trampling of Jerusalem by gentile powers, (**Revelation 11:2**) and for the rule of the Beast. (**Revelation 13:5**) The ministry of the two witnesses is also given as 1260 days. (**Revelation 11:3**) What we are looking at here is the time span of the Great Tribulation which is the second half of those seven years of Daniel's 70th week.

Up ahead in the fall season of some future year the road narrows. The 'Highway of Holiness' awaits the passage of God's faithful witnesses. At some point in the future they will come into the end-time drama. Even now the end-time pilgrims are preparing to finish the race. That epic journey began with their father Abraham, father of the faithful. They will finish the journey he began 4,000 years ago. (**Isaiah 35:8-10**)

Desertion in the face of danger, dereliction of duty, and in military parlance "going A.W.O.L" or "absent without leave" is an awful thing. Abandonment is abhorrent to both God and man. This is amply demonstrated in the Acts 27 account of the shipwreck of the Apostle Paul. The Apostle Paul also warns us that there will be an apostasy, an abandonment of the faith by many in the end time. Here is the Word of God.

(**Thessalonians 2:3-4**) "*Let no man deceive you by any means: for that Day shall not come, except there some a falling away first, (apostasy), and that man of sin be revealed, the son of perdition; Who opposeth and exalteth himself above all that is called god, or worshipped; so that he as God sitteth in the temple of God, shewing himself that he is God.*"

Daniel also shows us quite clearly that the coming 70th week of Daniel will involve a 7 year covenant entered into by "many" in the household of God.

(**Daniel 9:27**) "*And he shall confirm the covenant with many for one week: and in the midst of the week he shall cause the sacrifice and the oblation to cease, and for the overspreading of abominations he shall make it desolate, even until the consummation, and that determined shall be poured upon the desolate.*"

They will go down to make a deal with a coming prince, a prince who is not the true Messiah but a false one. Yes "many" in the Judeo-Christian family of Abraham, Isaac and Jacob will go to the table of the coming prince of darkness and make covenant with this apparent global mega-dealer. This is an awful truth but God always warns His covenant people of things to come. The initial ploy of this false prince is to present himself as a global peacemaker and power broker. He will apparently sell the deal as a temporary borrowing of power from the kings and national rulers, especially of the G-7 nations. He will probably say that this 7 year sovereignty sharing treaty with the western nations is just an "emergency measure" to be taken just temporarily until the Utopian vision of a New World Order can be firmly established. This future great world leader will assume power by means of a sovereignty sharing treaty with Israel and the G-7/G-8 nations. This prince who is to come may even promise to hand back the political power to the rulers of the nations at the end of the 7 years. But during that time he will reveal himself to be a false messiah. He will be the coming prince of darkness prophesied to come in the apocalyptic passages of the Holy Scriptures. Basically he says to Israel, "Trust me! Just give me the power and I will set things right. Then I will fix up the world and return it to you."

What a lie that will be! Yet the nations will have no choice. They have stated publicly that internationalism needs a "strong hand from somewhere". They believe in man. They are Utopians. They are humanists, and this means both secular humanists and religious humanists. They believe a man with charisma can initiate the humanistic dream of a New World Order. They desperately want to see it firmly established. With nuclear disarmament, and the assurance of middle east and global 'peace and security', freedom from hunger, world health, etc. All these world programs need strong central leadership. Global economic equality, global warming, and global eco-salvation are burning issues that they believe can be addressed by this "strong leadership". And so they await 'the man'.

The dream of achieving this man centered Utopian happiness (without God) is not new. It goes back a long way. It hails from the ancient post flood Tower of Babel. At that time Nimrod and his mother/wife Semiramis attempted to gather the peoples under one humanistic politico-religious covering. Of course they left God out of the picture. And so they failed.

But the dream lives on in the humanistic pantheistic heart. It has been fostered down through time by a host of hidden entities which I won't go into here. Beatle John Lennon reignited this dream some years back with his song, "Imagine".

So the world is waiting for this to happen. All that is required is the appropriate crisis and the emergence of the prophesied "crisis manager" onto the stage of history. The Bible tells us about this in. (**Daniel 9:27**) this humanistic covenant with "many" is what initiates the final seven years of God's determined dealings with His Jewish and Christian people. These are all the people who claim allegiance to the God of Abraham, Isaac, and Jacob.

The coming world history will not be a pleasant time for people of conscience and Christian devotion. Many will fall away from the faith in the coming great apostasy spoken of by our Apostle Paul. But we can rejoice in this one thing. God is in control. He sets the agenda of holy history. In all of this God's sovereign purposes will overrule. When all is said and done, God will bring forth the remnant of His people in a victorious deliverance and return. They will be refined as gold and Messiah will return in vengeance and deliverance of His people at a place (or places) knowable spiritually as, the "sheep-pens" of "Bozrah". – (**Micah 2:12-13**) As we come up to the last days of this age Jerusalem will be delivered, the Jewish nation will be saved. (**Zechariah 12:7; 13:1**) And the gospel will have been preached to the ends of the earth.

So that being said, let us face the facts of Holy Scripture. We are told that "many", (which we must assume will include God's people of interest Israel and Christendom), will make this 7 year covenant with this "prince" spoken of by the prophet Daniel. Here they will "take the low road". They will abandon their hopes, their faith, and their love for the coming Messiah. Instead they will turn aside to begin a walk with a global mega-dealer/peacemaker.

We know how all this will end up. In the very same verse Daniel tells us that this prince will step out of his guise as peacemaker and reveal himself half way through the 7 years covenant he will then be seen as the Beast or Antichrist. (**Daniel 9:27**) To go with the man at this point will call for total commitment. He will call for, (and insist on), absolute surrender and obedience to himself and his 666 economic system. Any man or woman who enters into his 666 initiation and into his worship ceremony will be entering into total and absolute apostasy with no hope of redemption.

At the beginning of the 7 years it will be nice. Duped members of the political and religious institutions of mankind will sit down at table and make deals with this man. Of course he will be the ultimate agent of humanism. And 20th century history showcased such absolutist leaders in Stalin, Hitler, Mao Tse Tung, and Pol Pot. So we know what we can expect from godless humanistic leadership. But men who deny God are fools. (**Proverbs 1**) They prefer to make a deal with a crook rather than cry out to God for His covering of grace. Thus they will begin their desertion. As they make this 7-year deal they will begin to turn away from YHVH/God and the way of holiness. They deny God and the power of His everlasting covenant. Of course many during those first 3.5 years will see the light, change their mind, and turn back to God. Others will proclaim the

Kingdom of God right from that very moment. These faithful ones will go forth as the Anabaptists did and proclaim Christ/Messiah as their only King. They will operate without political protection. Thus begins the end-time drama.

This is a blockbuster piece of information. How we respond on that epic coming day of apostasy will be a matter of life and death. This will be the ultimate collision between the Eternal Covenant in Jesus Christ and this ultimate covenant of end-time humanism. The professors of 'higher criticism' have always hated the book of Daniel and sought to discredit it. And partial preterism today seeks to twist its meaning. So now we can begin to realize why such a battle is raging over this one little scripture in (**Daniel 9:27**).

Daniel was a man of prayer and fasting. He sought the face of God on behalf of His people. This includes his Jewish people and also us in the true church which overflowed out of Israel back 2000 years ago on the Day of Pentecost. We are also the congregation of God, the Elect, the ones 'called out' as an "ecclesia" to be the people in whom the promised Seed of Abraham is to reside. (**Galatians 3:29**)

So as we can see, Daniel brought to us a huge amount of critical information on the last days. This information relates heavily to the Gentile powers and how they will behave throughout history and right up into the final 7 years of this age. God gave us this information. It is critical information for the saints as they pilgrim on to Zion. It is absolutely essential that we get it right. God forbid that we are led astray by religious wheeler-dealers, to find ourselves slipping and sliding down a precipice into apostasy.

(**Daniel 9:27**) is the key scripture for us to understand. It is essential for our understanding of the end times. It is the threshold into the 70th week of Daniel. This verse is an enormously important signpost on the pilgrim pathway. A veritable swarm of dark spirits is discharging a fog of disinformation over this verse. Preterits heretics are saying that the "covenant" in (**Daniel 9:27**) relates to the holy covenant. They say that it was fulfilled in the life of Christ or was totally fulfilled back in the first century. To any solid faithful study of these verses such a notion is patently untrue. The (**Daniel 9:27**) "covenant" is dark and dirty. There is nothing holy about it. The latter part of the very same verse shows that this 7 year deal is cut by someone who goes on to become an abominator and one who leads many into apostasy.

As we can see this is a revealing piece of information. It raises the curtains to reveal the crucial scenes of the drama at the end of this age. It sets the scene for the final act of the play. This is a not a holy covenant being referred to here. It is a very earthy one. Daniel is showcasing a future time when a covenant people who should know better give a man complete and total global dictatorial rule. It is authoritarian politics on an international scale. And they suffer for it. They end up in a Great Tribulation.

And where do we as Christian believers figure in all this?

Well during our lifetime we ourselves may be the ones going up onto that stage when that curtain opens. We had best take the early opportunity we have right now to prepare our hearts. Because in the midst of this darkness God's Light will shine forth in the nations. (**Isaiah 60**) We need the Holy Spirit's infilling. We need to find the oil for our lamps against the coming night.

6 DECEPTION IN THE LAST DAYS

Paul tells us specifically what the "unrighteous deception" in (**2 Thessalonians 2:10**) is for which the people depart. In verse 7, he names it "*the mystery of lawlessness,*" a set of beliefs that is totally contrary to "*the truth*" (verses 10-12). This deception is "*the lie*" that Satan has always foisted on mankind—that we do not need to obey God's law, see (**Genesis 3:4; Romans 1:21-25**).

Are These the Last Days?

The apostle Paul prophesies of an apostasy in (**2 Thessalonians 2:3, 9-12**), and he prefaces it with a warning against being deceived. The great apostasy may already be fully underway, spurred by the rising tide of deception in society. With so much information available—along with so many ways to manipulate it—men find it extremely easy to deceive millions instantly. This is especially true for those who do not really believe the true source of knowledge, God and His Word. Thus, after subtle doctrinal changes, many of the brethren have fallen away.

The "coming of the lawless one," however, is still future. His rise to prominence and power will be accompanied by incredible miracles, but they will be false signs and wonders, lies produced by Satan to appear as if they are of God see (**Revelation 13:11-15**). He will use "*all unrighteous deception,*" a hint that what he does and says will appear as righteous, yet someone who knows and loves the truth can see through it and avoid being deceived.

Satan will really pull out all the stops to deceive as many as possible, especially the called sons of God. The "lawless one" will be so slick that "*And all that dwell upon the earth shall worship him, whose names are not written in the Book of Life of the Lamb slain from the foundation of the world.*" (**Revelation 13:8**)

But, as Paul writes elsewhere, if we hold fast to "the pattern of sound words" that we learned, if we guard the truth, we will not be deceived.

Paul repeats these instructions to the Thessalonians in this context:

(**2 Thessalonians 2:15**) *"Therefore, brethren, stand fast and hold the traditions which ye have been taught, whether by word or epistle."*

The key to resisting deception is being convicted of the truth! The truth is what was first revealed to the apostles. As Jude puts it:

(**Jude 1:3**)*"Beloved, when I gave all diligence to write unto you of the common salvation, it was needful for me to write unto you, and exhort you that ye should earnestly contend for the faith which was once delivered unto the saints."*

As they saw the first-century apostasy coming, all the apostles warn about deceivers and urge the brethren to be certain of and stick to the doctrines of God. It is our surest hedge against being caught up in the deceptions of the end time that are already upon us.

Deceptions of the End Time

(**2 Thessalonians 2:3**) *"Let no man deceive you by any means: for* that day shall not come, *except there come a falling away first, and that man of sin be revealed, the son of perdition;"*

People fall away because they do not have the love of the truth. Consequently, they have nothing to pour out their energies on, and so they drift away. Anybody who is drifting will follow the current opinion within the body, whatever it happens to be.

Don't Be a Prudent Agnostic

Paul wrote 2nd Thessalonians to correct their false impression by telling them what Christ had revealed to him regarding the "*gathering together with Christ*" of those dead in Christ and those remaining alive when He returned. He opens by telling them, first of all, that Christ's return will be preceded by a period of apostasy that could include anything from a falling away, a departure from doctrine or teaching, all the way to and including an outright political rebellion.

The second sign would be the appearance of the man of sin. This person has four different names or titles, but all of them are described similarly: *the man of sin* (**2 Thessalonians 2:3-10**), *the little horn* (**Daniel 7:8**), *the two-horned* *lamb who spoke like a dragon* (**Revelation 13:11-18**), and *the false prophet* (**Revelation 19:20**). The description in each location is not exactly alike, but each adds to what the other gives. Consider this summary of comparisons.

In each case, the person described appears at the time of the end. This is the one piece of information that every one of them has in common.

- In three of the four, his end—his destruction or annihilation—comes at the return of Jesus Christ (**Daniel 7:8-9; 2 Thessalonians 2:3; Revelation 19:20**).
- In three of the four, it directly states or strongly implies the person speaks with great pompous words (**Daniel 7:8-9; 2 Thessalonians 2:4; Revelation 13:11-14**).
- In three of the four, it directly states the person does miraculous, supernatural signs (**II Thessalonians 2:9; Revelation 13:13-15; Revelation 19:20**).
- In two of them, the signs are done in the presence of the Beast, showing they are not the same figure (**Revelation 13:13-15; 19:20**).
- In two of them, he deceives and leads people into idolatry (**2 Thessalonians 2:4-10; Revelation 13:12, 14**).
- In two of them, he either makes war against the saints or causes those who would not worship the beast to be put to death (**Daniel 7:21; Revelation 13:15**).
- In two of them, he either thinks to change times and law—suggesting the law of God—or he sets himself in the Temple of God, proclaiming himself to be God. The implication is that he has the authority to do these things (**Daniel 7:25; 2 Thessalonians 2:4**).
- In two of them, his period of greatest influence is three and a half years (**Daniel 7:25; Revelation 13:5**).

All of these scriptures are describing the same person. The Bible shows that this person—the man of sin—has a direct connection to a large political power and has a religious influence. It should be understood that we are dealing with a personage and with prophecies of *global* significance.

A Place of Safety?

(**2 Thessalonians 2:13-14**) *"But we are bound to give thanks always to God for you, brethren beloved of the Lord, because God hath from the beginning chosen you to salvation through sanctification of the Spirit and belief of the truth: Whereunto he called you by our gospel, to the obtaining of the glory of our Lord Jesus Christ."*

Sanctification is just the opposite of apostasy. Apostasy means "to depart" from truth, and from God. Sanctification, on the other hand, is becoming more attached to God until Christ's image is formed in us. There is a contrast, then, between those condemned and those who are going to receive salvation, which will be rescued because they love the truth.

A Place of Safety?

(**1 Timothy 6:20**) *"O Timothy, keep that which is committed to thy trust, avoiding profane and vain babblings, and oppositions of science falsely so called."*

In Paul's letters to Timothy, he urges the young evangelist in the strongest of terms to stand firm and to hold fast to the doctrine that the apostle had given to him. (**1 Timothy 6:20**) Paul needs to warn him because; by about AD 65, the church is already sliding away from the truth that Jesus Christ had entrusted to the apostles.

Why is doctrine so important to God? Why does He not want his people to deviate from what He spoke in His Word? The answer is basic and simple: Deviation from orthodoxy will not produce the right fruit in fulfilling His purpose.

God makes allowances, of course, for minor variations. Not everyone will have the same level of obedience or understanding. Not everyone is equally wise or educated. However, His people will have a strong belief in the doctrines most important and central to His purpose. If these central doctrines are missing, then the deviations that are present will endanger the purpose He is working out.

Perhaps the analogy of following a recipe in the baking of a cake will suffice to show the principles involved in keeping doctrine pure. If in baking a cake, a baker left out certain ingredients, or if he added others that the recipe did not call for, or if he used the right ingredients but in the wrong proportions, it is entirely possible with any of these combinations not even to end up with a cake! Obviously, to produce a perfect cake, one must use the right ingredients in the right proportions.

Though this is certainly an ideal, God wants His people to aim for it because of His purpose. One may never hit such a high target, but that does not relieve one of the burdens of striving to develop the right proportion of the right ingredients in every part of life. (**Ephesians 4:13**) says, "*Till we all come in the unity of the faith, and of the knowledge of the Son of God, unto a perfect man, unto the measure of the stature of the fullness of Christ.*"

The called of God have a tremendously high purpose and hope: to be gods! The Bible unequivocally states that we are to be like Him, that is, like Jesus Christ (**1 John 3:2**) "Beloved, now are we the sons of God, and it doth not yet appear what we shall be: but we know that, when he shall appear, we shall be like him; for we shall see him as he is." It follows that the ingredients that produce that potential be as close to perfect as possible.

Guard the Truth!

(2 Timothy 1:13-14) *"Who was before a blasphemer, and a persecutor, and injurious: but I obtained mercy, because I did it ignorantly in unbelief. And the grace of our Lord was exceeding abundant with faith and love which is in Christ Jesus."*

He tells Timothy—and every Christian—to hold to the standards that the apostle had delivered to him. And, he says, the only way to keep the doctrines is both to live it and proclaim it with faith and love. Paul is concerned, not just about the truth, but also about how it is preserved, in faith and love. Regarding keeping the deposit through God's Holy Spirit, The Expositor's Bible Commentary states, "It has been well said that the Holy Spirit is the great Conservator of orthodoxy". In other words, a person led by and using the Spirit of God will not turn away from the teaching delivered by the apostles.

(2 Timothy 2:16-18) *"But shun profane and vain babblings: for they will increase unto more ungodliness. And their word will eat as doth a canker: of whom is Hymenaeus and Philetus; Who concerning the truth have erred, saying that the resurrection is past already; and overthrow the faith of some."*

The metaphor changes from cutting a road (verse 15) to shooting an arrow at a target. The word of truth, the gospel, is the target. If you shoot an arrow at a target, one of three things will happen:

1. The arrow will hit the bull's-eye;
2. It will go slightly off, left or right, top or bottom, still hitting somewhere within the target area;
3. It will miss the target completely.

Some Bibles translate verse 18 as "who have swerved", "wandered away", or "erred" from the truth. None of these translations are complete in capturing the metaphor. When you shoot an arrow, it goes straight, but not necessarily straight at the target! If you watch someone else shoot an arrow, where are your eyes pointing? Do they not follow the arrow to the target? That is the point. The arrow is the teaching that the teacher gives, and no matter how straight he gives it, if he is not aiming directly at the bull's-eye and hitting it, his students eyes will not be on the right goal!

The weight of responsibility is heavy on the minister. Not only is he to give instruction that is plain and clear, he is also to give instruction that is right on target so people do not get distracted by false doctrine. A minister can be perfectly sincere, but if he points his teaching toward the wrong goal, he will miss the target. Fortunately, our God is faithful and makes every effort to turn us toward the right goal.

These metaphors and illustrations show how important doctrine and having the right gospel are. Doctrine forms belief; belief determines action and character. Minimizing the future aspects of the gospel alters our vision of where we are going with our lives. The future aspects of the gospel cannot be demoted in priority to second or third place without seriously compromising our Christian lives since it removes the right goal and deflects people away from the Kingdom of God. When people are deflected from the right goal, the teaching of the gospel changes and God's creative process begins to wind down and may even stop entirely.

God is concerned about doctrine because it determines what a person is now and will be in the future. As one lives it, it becomes more ingrained in his life and will eventually become indelibly stamped on his character. Then God has a choice, either to give him immortality, or consign him to the Lake of Fire. Regardless of how straight we pursue our objectives in life, if we are aimed at the wrong goal, we cannot produce the kind of life—the character—that God wants in His Kingdom. Correct doctrine is eternally vital!

(**Hebrews 2:1-4**) "*Therefore we ought to give the more earnest heed to the things which we have heard, lest at any time we should let* them *slip. For if the word spoken by angels was steadfast, and every transgression and disobedience received a just recompense of reward; How shall we escape, if we neglect so great salvation; which at the first began to be spoken by the Lord, and was confirmed unto us by them that heard* him*; God also bearing* them *witness, both with signs and wonders, and with divers miracles, and gifts of the Holy Ghost, according to his own will?*"

Paul's warning to the Hebrews here is a bit stronger than what he says in (**Philippians 1:27**). He says there, "*Only let your conversation be as it becometh the gospel of Christ: that whether I come and see you, or else be absent, I may near of your affairs, that ye stand fast in one sprit, with one mind striving together token of perdition, but to you of salvation, and that of God*". Here he says, "Give earnest heed to the doctrine, to the gospel, to the things we heard, because we're in danger of losing it!" He feels he must frighten them, saying, "Don't you remember that under the Mosaic dispensation people were punished very severely for neglecting what they had heard? Every transgression and disobedience received a just reward. How much greater under the dispensation through Christ, the Son?" He is quite serious. Work hard. Be diligent. Make your calling sure!

It is about this same time that Peter and Jude add their voices to his. The brethren were undergoing a rough time because false ministers and false teachers were in the church, and like us, they also had to fight off the pressures from the world to conform. It takes great effort to resist both in the church and out in the world. When there are problems among us, it is tough. When we must also resist all the downward pulls outside in society, it is a difficult, sore trial. Thus, Paul uses particularly strong language to motivate them to stand up, face the problem, give it their all, and vanquish it.

Are we in a similar circumstance? Perhaps some of the details are different; the deception has taken a somewhat different form (this time we do not have to contend with Gnosticism, per se). However, there is enough similarity that warnings here, as well as in the books of Peter, John, and Jude, make a lot of sense. Certainly the results, the fruit of false teaching, are the same: apostasy, falling away, confusion, distrust (especially of those who have been given a measure of authority, the ministry), scattering, and disunity. The apostles, then, are speaking to us.

(**Hebrews 10:19-20**) "*Having therefore, brethren, boldness to enter into the holiest by the blood of Jesus, By a new and living way, which he hath consecrated for us, through the veil, that is to say, his flesh,*"

(**Hebrews 10:19**) begins the verbal bridge that transitions from the doctrinal material to its practical application. This latter section contains arguably the most powerful exhortations in the entire Bible for us to get up and get going. If these Hebrews were not Laodicean as a whole, they were very close to it.

Overall, God is saying through the apostle, "Don't you realize your danger? Being justified and sanctified, you absolutely cannot allow yourselves to continue in your neglectful ways. You have powerful help available through Christ, yet you are drifting away! Don't you realize what you are giving up by your slow but steady drift into apostasy?" He had already warned them as chapter 2 opened that their neglect of their privileges and responsibilities was allowing this great salvation to slip away.

In (**Hebrews 10:19**), He reminds them that they already have access to God, so they should come before Him with eager boldness. This is one of our great privileges. Adam and Eve were kicked out of the Garden and God's presence, but through Christ, God's regenerated children are now invited into His presence in spirit. Because the way has been prepared for us to do this, we are able to come to know God up close and personal. This is among the greatest of all blessings afforded to everyone who makes the New Covenant.

In other words, He meets with us, not outside the back or front door, but inside the house! And not merely inside the house but inside the second room beyond the veil—the Holy of Holies—where formerly only the High Priest was welcome once a year! The veil separating the rooms in the Temple was torn asunder at Christ's death *"And, behold, the veil of the temple was rent in twain from the top to the bottom; and the earth did quake, and the rocks rent;"* (**Matthew 27:51**). Nothing hinders our liberty to go boldly into God's very throne room.

Jesus Christ Himself is "the Way" to the Father *"Jesus saith unto him, I am the way, the truth, and the life: no man cometh unto the Father, but by me."* (**John 14:6**). As High Priest, Jesus has dedicated Himself to intercede on behalf of us sinners in our relations with God. In (**John 17:19**), in His prayer the night before His crucifixion, He says, *"And for their* [His disciples'] *sakes I sanctify Myself, that they also might be sanctified through the truth."* He set Himself apart to the shedding of His blood for us and to His position as our High Priest.

The phrase in (**Hebrews 10:20**), "through the veil, that is, His flesh," refers to what He did as a human to make this access to God possible. When He was flesh and blood, He died for us so that we, like Him, could go directly into the Holy of Holies. Spiritually, His death pierced the veil.

(**Hebrews 10:23**) *"Let us hold fast the profession of our faith without wavering; (for he is faithful that promised ;)"*

God's power: our shield against apostasy

(**Hebrews 10:23**) *"let us hold fast the profession of our faith without wavering; (for he is faithful that promised;)"*

Let us hold fast the confession of our hope - This is Paul's reason for writing the epistle. They were enduring great pressure to relax their standards. Some were beginning to return to their former beliefs and to the world. Apostasy had begun to set in.

Today in the confusion of the times, we cannot allow our foundations to be chipped away by listening to the myriad of differing opinions and beliefs. So many voices babble incessantly, each one trying to get our attention that they can nearly drive us mad with confusion! Confusion not only affects what we believe but also our zeal for God's way of life. It is imperative we *"earnestly contend for the faith which was once for all delivered to the saints"*. (**Jude 1:3**)

Jesus gives us this warning in His messages to the Thyatira, Sardis, and Philadelphia churches: *"But hold fast what you have till I come. . . . Remember therefore how you have received and heard; hold fast, and repent . . . Behold, I come quickly! Hold that fast which thou hast, that no man take thy crown"* see (**Revelation 2:25; 3:3, 11**).

It is of paramount importance to keep a firm grip on the true teachings of God's Word.

Contend Earnestly

(**Hebrews 10:25**) "*Not forsaking the assembling of ourselves together, as the manner of some is; but exhorting one another: and so much the more, as ye see the day approaching.*

We have now reached one of the most solemn and fear-provoking sections of Scripture. We need to understand that this passage is written to Christians, not to the world, and what it threatens is facing any Christian who does not choose to believe that God is serious. God is thundering at His own children because some of them have become insipidly blasé about what He has done for them and have ignored the help that He makes so readily available to them.

This does not mean that everybody who heard this message was in that perilous spiritual condition. It was given, however, against the backdrop of some having already departed from the church, and it uses them as examples of what not to do, for the purpose of warning the others about what those who left are facing. To determine just where he stands, each person has to examine himself in light of Paul's instruction.

Yet, some who heard this message had regressed so far that they were on track to apostatize, which means "to depart from the faith." This subject is Paul's major motivation for writing the letter. He first introduces it as early as (**Hebrews 3:12**): "*Take heed, brethren, lest there be in any of you an evil heart of unbelief, in departing from the living God.*" "Departing" is the Greek word aphistemi, meaning "to remove" or "to instigate to revolt."

How far had people departed? (**Hebrews 10:25**) gives a clear indication by Paul's use of the word "forsaking" regarding assembling on the Sabbath. The Greek word means exactly this: Some of the Hebrews were not missing just an occasional Sabbath service but had abandoned attending Sabbath services entirely for extended periods, if not altogether. This accounts for the strength of the apostle's message.

A similar passage in (**2 Peter 2:20-22**) reads: "*For if after they have escaped the pollutions of the world through the knowledge of the Lord and Savior Jesus Christ, they are again entangled therein, and overcome, the latter end is worse for them than the beginning. For it would have been better for them not to have known the way of righteousness, than having known it, to turn from the holy commandment delivered to them. But it has happened to them according to the true proverb: The dog is turned to his own vomit again; and the sow that was washed, to her wallowing in the mire.*"

Peter speaks of apostasy here. He says it would have been better had they never known the way of righteousness rather than know it and then turn from it. Jesus said of Judas that it would have been better for him not to have been born (**Matthew 26:24**). The same end faced those who had forsaken assembling together on the Sabbath.

(**1 Timothy 1:19**) "*Holding faith, and a good conscience; which some having put away concerning faith have made shipwreck:*"

This contains a vivid illustration of apostasy, saying that an apostate makes shipwreck of his faith in God. Having escaped the world, he returns to it and soon finds himself on the rocks, being beaten to death by the waves of life. As mentioned earlier, a person does not apostatize in one giant leap. Just as the Israelites obtained the Promised Land step by step, so apostasy occurs step by step. One goes forward, the other backward. If the backslider takes appropriate action, he does not have to lose his faith.

God's Power: Our Shield Against Apostasy

(**Hebrews 10:26-27**) "*For if we sin willfully after that we have received the knowledge of the truth, there remaineth no more sacrifice for sins, But a certain fearful looking for of judgment and fiery indignation, which shall devour the adversaries.*"

The first thing to note in (**Hebrews 10:26-27**) is the word "sin." Paul is not speaking of sin in general but the specific sin of apostasy from the faith that was once known and professed. The apostasy he has in mind is not so much an act but a state brought on by many individual attitudes and sins, reproducing the original, carnal antagonism a person has toward God before conversion.

Some commentaries insist that the Authorized Version is not quite correct in translating the term in verse 26 as "willfully." These argue that the Greek word, hekousios, will not permit this translation. It appears only one other time, in (**1 Peter 5:2**), where it is translated as "willingly." The commentators insist that it should be rendered "willingly" in (**Hebrews 10:26**).

The American Heritage College Dictionary supports their conclusion. To do something *willfully* is to do it purposely or deliberately. The commentators say all sin is done purposely because human nature is set up to do so, even though weakness, ignorance, or deception may be involved as well. To do a thing *willingly* is to be disposed, inclined, or prepared to do it. Its synonyms are "readily," "eagerly," "compliantly," "ungrudgingly," "voluntarily," and "volitionally." This sense is contained in the context because, by the time a person reaches the apostate stage in his backward slide, where he has forsaken God and His way, he has *no* resistance to sin.

The sinner is deliberately, even eagerly, determined to abandon Christ, to turn away from God and His way, having completely become an enemy once again. He sin's with barely a second thought, if with any thought at all. He sins automatically, as there is none of God's Spirit left to constrain him. His conscience is totally defiled; he has forsaken God.

Who is in danger of committing this sin? All who have made a profession of faith in Christ but are now neglecting their salvation.

The message of Hebrews is that it does not have to be this way. If the person takes heed and stirs himself awake, if he truly seeks to overcome and grow once again, if he returns to being a living sacrifice and seeking to glorify God, if he truly denies himself and takes up his cross, if he keeps God's commandments to live life as a Christian, he will *not* apostatize.

He may fall back from time to time, but as long as he repents and honestly seeks God when sin occurs in his life, the sin is readily forgiven. (**I John 1:9**) confidently proclaim, "*If we confess our sins, He is faithful and just to forgive us our sins and to cleanse us from all unrighteousness.*" (**John 14:23**) assures us that as long as we are keeping His Word, we are safe. "*Jesus answered and said unto him, If a man love me, he will keep my words: and my Father will love him, and we will come unto him, and make our abode with him.*"

(**Hebrews 12:5-10**) explains that God is faithfully working in our behalf, even chastening us if He sees fit, to get us turned around and headed again in the right direction and attitude. He does this faithfully because He does not want to lose us. Christ died for each child of God, thus each child He loves - and He loves them all - represents a substantial investment. Christ did not die in vain for anybody. In (**Hebrews 13:5c**), He charges us with the task of putting to work His promise, "*I will never leave you nor forsake you.*"

God's Power: Our Shield Against Apostasy

(**2 Peter 1:10-11**) "*Wherefore the rather, brethren, give diligence to make your calling and election sure: for if ye do these things, ye shall never fall: For so an entrance shall be ministered unto you abundantly into the everlasting kingdom of our Lord and Saviour Jesus Christ.*"

For those who believe in the doctrine of eternal security, (**2 Peter 1:10-11**) is a particularly difficult passage to dispute because it exposes the lie in this infernal teaching. It does this by stating a simple command that God asks us to carry out.

The inverse is also true; if we fail to do what Peter advises, then our calling and election are not sure. Beyond that, if we stumble, an entrance will not be supplied to us into the Kingdom of God.

God has done His part. He called or elected us out of all the billions on this planet. He forgave us, granted us repentance, and gave us His Holy Spirit. He opened up the truth to us and revealed Himself and His way of life to us. He made the New Covenant with us, supplying us with spiritual gifts, love, and faith. There is no end to what He has done for us.

Nevertheless, if we do not reciprocate, the relationship He has begun will fall apart. Our calling and election are not certain without us doing our part. We can fall away and not make it into the Kingdom of God.

Why did Peter write this to the whole church (verse 1)? He wrote it because the church at the time was experiencing various apostasies. (**2 Peter 2:3**) False teachers were bringing into the church destructive doctrines to turn the people away.

Why would Satan put false teachers in the church if there was no chance for the people to fall away? If church members have eternal security, why waste his time on them? However, Satan himself knows that Christians do not have eternal security, and he tries his best to turn us into apostates. We can fall away!

Peter was writing in this atmosphere. The people in the first-century church were living in a time of false teachings, false teachers, and apostasy, and he needed to warn them.

(**2 Peter 1:12**) "*Wherefore I will not be negligent to put you always in remembrance of these of these things, though ye know them, and are established in the present truth.*"

This, too, begs the question: Why did Peter command them to make their calling and election sure? If they had the truth, and he admitted that they were established in it, why did they have to make it "sure"? In making their calling and election sure, they would be doing the one thing that would keep them on the right path to the Kingdom. Christians keep themselves from falling into deception, error, and sin - keep themselves from apostatizing and losing their salvation - by validating their conversion.

When a thing is validated, it is objectively determined to be genuine, true, real, authentic, or legitimate. How do Christians validate their calling and election? The answer is simple. Jesus describes it in (**Matthew 7:16-20**). We validate our calling and election by producing fruit. Jesus expounds on this in His Passover message in:

(**John 15**) "*I am the true vine, and my Father is the husbandman. Every branch in me that beareth not fruit he taketh away: and every branch that beareth fruit, he purgeth it, that it may bring forth more fruit. Now ye are clean through the word which I have spoken unto you. Abide in me, and I in you. As the branch cannot bear fruit of itself, except it abide in the vine; no more can ye, except ye abide in me. I am the vine, ye are the branches: He that abideth in me, and I in him, the same bringeth forth much fruit: for without me ye can do nothing. If a man abide not in me, he is cast forth as a branch, and is withered; and men gather them, and cast them into the fire, and they are burned. If ye abide in me, and my words abide in you, ye shall ask what ye will, and it shall be done unto you. Herein is my Father glorified, that ye bear much fruit; so shall ye be my*" *disciples. As the Father hath loved me, so have I loved you: continue ye in my love. If ye keep my commandments, ye shall abide in my love; even as I have kept my Father's commandments, and abide in his love. These things have I spoken unto you, that my joy might remain in you, and that your joy might be full. This is my commandment, That ye love one another, as I have loved you. Greater love hath no man than this that a man lay down his life for his friends. Ye are my friends, if ye do whatsoever I command you.*"

The Vine and the Branches

(**John 15 :15-27**) "*Henceforth I call you not servants; for the servant knoweth not what his lord doeth: but I have called you friends; for all things that I have heard of my Father I have made known unto you. Ye have not chosen me, but I have chosen you, and ordained you, that ye should go and bring forth fruit, and that your fruit should remain: that whatsoever ye shall ask of the Father in my name, he may give it you. These things I command you, that ye love one another. If the world hate you, ye know that it hated me before it hated you. If ye were of the world, the world would love his own: but because ye are not of the world, but I have chosen you out of the world, therefore the world hateth you. Remember the word that I said unto you, The servant is not greater than his lord. If they have persecuted me, they will also persecute you; if they have kept my saying, they will keep yours also. But all these things will they do unto you for my name's sake, because they know not him that sent me. If I had not come and spoken unto them, they had not had sin: but now they have no cloke for their sin. He that hateth me hateth my Father also. If I had not done among them the works which none other man did, they had not had sin: but now have they both seen and hated both me and my Father. But this cometh to pass, that the word might be fulfilled that is written in their law, They hated me without a cause. But when the Comforter is come, whom I will send unto you from the Father, even the Spirit of truth, which proceedeth from the Father, he shall testify of me: And ye also shall bear witness, because ye have been with me from the beginning.*"

This blows the eternal security doctrine to smithereens. Our Savior, Jesus Christ - our Judge - says that if we do not bear fruit, God will take us away and throw us into the fire! If we bear fruit, however, we will glorify the Father and truly be disciples of Christ, that is, true Christians!

We validate our calling by growing in grace and knowledge. "*But grow in grace, and in the knowledge of our Lord and Saviour Jesus Christ. To him be glory both now and forever. Amen.*" (**2 Peter 3:18**). If we are showing love to the brethren, if we are serving as opportunity permits, if we are deepening our relationship with God, we can be certain that our calling and election are still firmly in force.

Do We Have 'Eternal Security'?

(**2 Peter 2:1-3**) *"But there were false prophets also among the people, even as there shall be false teachers among you, who privily shall bring in damnable heresies, even denying the Lord that bought them, and bring upon themselves swift destruction. And many shall follow their pernicious ways; by reason of whom the way of truth shall be evil spoken of. And through covetousness shall they with feigned words make merchandise of you: whose judgment now of a long time lingereth not, and their damnation slumbereth not."*

These verses show us in a general way that traitors will come from within the church and subvert many to follow their carnal ways. Peter uses the word "but" to provide a contrast with the preceding section about the "sure word of prophecy" (**2 Peter 1:19**). These traitors to the faith are not led by the Holy Spirit as were those God inspired to write the prophecies (verse 21). The apostle immediately warns that these "false teachers" will come from within the church, or as Peter writes, "among you." The implication is that "forewarned is forearmed"! Therefore, be on guard!

Damnable Heresies

(**2 Peter 2:1**) *"But there were false prophets also among the people, even as there shall be false teachers among you, who privily shall bring in damnable heresies, even denying the Lord that bought them, and bring upon themselves swift destruction."*

Alarming as (**2 Peter 2:1-3**) is, Peter does not define heresy, but he does tell what one heresy is and will be. He also does not tell us here what the source of heresy is either.

Heresy is the translation of the Greek heresies—meaning literally "choice" or "selection"—which has an interesting secular as well as biblical history. Until its biblical use, it had no evil connotation. Even in the Bible, it is mostly used to refer to a party or a philosophy with which a person had chosen to identify or ally himself. Thus, heresies are frequently translated "sect." In Acts, Luke applies it to the Sadducees (**Acts 5:17**) and the Pharisees (**Acts 15:5; 26:5**). Outsiders also used heresies in (**Acts 24:5, 14 and Acts 28:22**) to identify the Christian church.

However, when Paul and Peter's writings began circulating, heresies meant a destructive element within the church that creates division through consciously formed opinions and ideas in disagreement with the orthodox teachings of the apostles. Paul condemns it in (**Galatians 5:20**) as one of "the works of the flesh." Sometimes it is translated "factions" or "party spirit," but regardless of its translation, Paul says that people who practice such things will not inherit the Kingdom of God!

In the ordinary course of secular life, heresy was of little consequence; one person's opinion or choice about most things in life is just as good as another's. A person can be given any number of alternatives, any one of which he may be perfectly free to believe. However, in Christianity we are dealing with revelation, with God-given truth, with absolutes. When God's truth comes to men, we either have to accept or reject it. Thus, a heretic is a man who believes what he wishes to believe instead of accepting the truth of God that he ought to believe.

(**2 Peter 2:1**) *"But there were false prophets also among the people, even as there shall be false teachers among you, who privily shall bring in damnable heresies, even denying the Lord that bought them, and bring upon themselves swift destruction."*

If "secretly" ("privily") were translated into the closest English synonym, it would have been rendered "smuggle." They smuggle in heresy by cunning deceit. The word literally means "they bring it along side," that is, they present this heresy in such a way as to make it appear favorably with the truth. "Oh, it's just a refinement. We're not really changing anything. You understand that, don't you? We're not really changing it. It's just a refinement, a clarification."

One denies the Lord by failing to submit to Him in obedience. If the doctrines gradually begin to be changed, then submission to Christ will be put in different terms as well.

(**2 Peter 2:1-2**) *"But there were false prophets also among the people, even as there shall be false teachers among you, who privily shall bring in damnable heresies, even denying the Lord that bought them, and bring upon themselves swift destruction. And many shall follow their pernicious ways; by reason of whom the way of truth shall be evil spoken of."*

Destructive will also translate into the English word "pernicious," which means "deadly." We hear it most frequently in a medical term, "pernicious anemia." What is so interesting is that it may appear innocent, but all the while it is destroying life. It gives the appearance of being not overtly or openly dangerous, but all the while it is undermining one's health. Peter, of course, is talking about spiritual health.

The King James Version calls their heresies damnable, implying that their words—their messages—are destructive to one's faith and relationship with God. "Denying the Lord" does not mean they deny that He lived or died or that He is God, but that their words and conduct are opposed to His fundamental nature. Their lives deny any close contact with Him.

What Is a False Prophet?

(**2 Peter 3:3-4**) *"Knowing this first, that there shall come in the last days scoffers, walking after their own lusts, And saying, Where is the promise of his coming? For since the fathers fell asleep, all things continue as they were from the beginning of the* *creation."*

Things are not continuing as they were, and the reason we know this is because God has given us discernment of the times and seasons in which we are living. Life is not going to continue the way it is: It will get worse before it gets better. So Peter is reminding us.

By the time Peter wrote this (scholars date 2 Peter in 64 AD); the world is in real turmoil. The world seemed to be falling apart. Jerusalem, especially, is a powder keg. Christians are being blamed for the trouble being incited in Rome.

However, the New Testament writers reveal to us that they saw the church going to sleep. We can imagine such a thing because many of us have experienced this in our own time. At the most critical juncture of history for the church, (**Matthew 25**) in the Parable of the Ten Virgins shows the church asleep—all ten were asleep, not just five of them. The parable specifically spotlights the virgins slumbering and sleeping at the time of the end, and it happened in the first century too, just before the destruction of the Temple, which was "an end."

It is an incongruity that seems almost impossible to believe. With all this excitement going on, instead of being stirred up to press on toward the Kingdom of God, the church instead—many of them anyway—were doing what the Thessalonians were doing, just waiting it out. Not everybody did that, and it is a good thing or Christianity would have died out.

The apostles were certainly stirred up. There is no doubt about it because they wrote about it. These people were doing exactly what the apostles were warning them of: They were walking after their own lusts or desires.

Don't Be a Prudent Agnostic

(**1 John 2:18-20**) *"Little children, it is the last time: and as ye have heard that antichrist shall come, even now are there many antichrists; whereby we know that it is the last time. They went out from us, but they were not of us; for if they had been of us, they would* no doubt *have continued with us: but* they *went out, that they might be made manifest that they were not all of us. But ye have an unction from the Holy One, and ye know all things."*

John informs us that the antichrists were right in the church fellowshipping with the truly converted! No doubt, they performed the same function in John's areas of responsibilities as they did in Paul's. They created a measure of havoc in the church through heretical teaching and then left the fellowship, proving they were not really part of the church. They were tares.

God's Sovereignty and the Church's Condition

(**1 John 2:18-19**) *"Little children, it is the last time: and as ye have heard that antichrist shall come, even now are there many antichrists; whereby we know that it is the last time. They went out from us, but they were not of us; for if they had been of us, they would no doubt have continued with us: but they went out, that they might be made manifest that they were not all of us."*

John calls the various individuals who were teaching heresy "antichrists." At one time, these people had fellowshipped with true believers, but then had left the church and were now trying to draw others away to follow their heretical teachings. John points out that they were never really converted, or they would have stayed with the body of true believers.

For the Perfecting of the Saints

(**Jude 1:2**) *"Mercy unto you, and peace, and love, be multiplied."*

Jude wishes upon his readers specific blessings. His salutation is not the same as the apostle Paul and some of the other writers used. He specifically chooses "mercy, peace, and love," as all three are vital in times of apostasy.

He asks for mercy because they probably needed to repent. His whole reason for writing the epistle stems from the fact that they had begun to get lax, allowing false teachers and false teachings in. They needed God's mercy as they began to repent.

He wishes them peace because, obviously, a major result of apostasy is war and division. Remember, his brother writes in (**James 3:18**) that the fruits of righteousness are produced in peace, and these people were not producing the fruits of righteousness for two reasons: false teachings and war. Thus, they needed peace.

(**James 3:18**) *"And the fruit of righteousness is sown in peace of them that make peace."*

Finally, he includes "love," the prime virtue. They needed love because it would take love to resolve this situation—and not just love for God but love for one another. This is the agape form of love, not just phileo— not just caring for one another but setting the mind to do God's will for each other and for God.

(**Jude 1:5-11**) *"I will therefore put you in remembrance, though ye once knew this, how that the Lord, having saved the people out of the land of Egypt, afterward destroyed them* *that believed not. And the angels which kept not their first estate, but left their own habitation, he hath reserved in everlasting chains under darkness unto the judgment of the great day. Even as Sodom and Gomorrah, and the cities about them in like manner, giving themselves over to fornication, and going after strange flesh, are set forth for an example, suffering the vengeance of eternal fire. Likewise also these* filthy *dreamers defile the flesh, despise dominion, and speak evil of dignities. Yet Michael the archangel, when contending with the devil he disputed about the body of Moses, durst not bring against him a railing accusation, but said, The Lord rebuke thee. But these speak evil of those things which they know not: but what they know naturally, as brute beasts, in those things they corrupt themselves. Woe unto them! For they have gone in the way of Cain, and ran greedily after the error of Balaam for reward, and perished in the gainsaying of Core."*

In these seven verses, Jude expands on his general description of false teachers in verse 4. He compares them in turn to the unbelieving Israelites, to the angels that sinned, and finally to the perverts in Sodom and vicinity. He is giving examples of the three major hallmarks of apostasy:

1. Unbelief, the Israelites' major failing.
2. Rebellion, which the angels who sinned did.
3. Immorality, what occurred in Sodom and Gomorrah?

Unbelief, rebellion, and immorality all result in divine judgment and punishment. The Israelites died in the wilderness, the angels that sinned were placed under restraint, and Sodom and Gomorrah were blasted off the face of the earth. We cannot find better examples of divine judgment and punishment than these.

(**Jude 1:11**) *"Woe unto them! For they have gone in the way of Cain, and ran greedily after the error of Balaam for reward, and perished in the gainsaying of Core."*

The apostle provides the examples of Cain, Balaam, and Korah as illustrative of apostates. All of them were rebellious and anti-God at the core but in different ways.

Cain's sin manifested itself in a sullen, selfish hatred that ended up in murder. Balaam's sin was manifested in the form of covetousness and greed, which he used to induce others to sin. (Recall that Jesus says)

(**Matthew 5:19**) *"Whosoever therefore shall break one of these least commandments, and shall teach men so, he shall be called the least in the kingdom of heaven: but whosoever shall do and teach them, the same shall be called great in the kingdom of heaven."*

So as we can see whoever teaches against God's law will be least in the Kingdom. These men may not even be there at all. Balaam certainly taught others to sin.

Korah's sin manifested itself in speaking against the God-appointed authority and attracting a following to wrest away an office that was not his. He is forever an example of that, reaching above his station, as it were. We do not hear much about rising above one's station in these democratic days, but the church is not a democratic society. The church is God's Family, and He places people in His body as it pleases Him (**I Corinthians 12:18**). Koran had been placed in Israel in a certain spot, and he tried to go above his station, persuading others to do the same and support him in his coup—and he ended up as a black spot in the wilderness of Sinai along with many of his supporters.

Jude, then, is not only showing sin, but also God's judgment and severe punishments for sin.

(**Revelation 2:2-3**) *"I know thy works, and thy labor, and thy patience, and how thou canst not bear them which are evil: and thou hast tried them which say they are apostles, and are not, and hast found them liars: And hast borne, and hast patience, and for my name's sake hast labored, and hast not fainted."*

Any saint who has sorted right from wrong doctrine, discerned good from evil leadership, and patiently continued to labor in Christ's name can identify with Ephesus! Identifying today's false apostles was not initially easy either, but many have seen how church leaders have turned true grace into lawlessness and voided God's law from their lives (**Jude 4; Psalm 119:126; Romans 3:31**). If we have continued in patience and good works, we can be encouraged by Christ's initial words to Ephesus, for they apply to us in principle, if not directly.

The Seven Churches: Ephesus

(**Revelation 2:3**) *"And hast borne, and hast patience, and for my name's sake hast labored, and hast not fainted."*

Jesus actually commends the Ephesians quite a bit. They had stood up to the falsehood and to the false teachers of the mid- to late-first century. Of course, He is speaking of the "core" group; the ones who were truly converted who stuck it out. They had seen who was false, and they avoided them.

(**Revelation 2:4-5**) *"Nevertheless I have somewhat against thee, because thou hast left thy first love. Remember therefore from whence thou art fallen, and repent, and do the* *first works; or else I will come unto thee quickly, and will remove thy candlestick out of his place, except thou repent."*

The Ephesians church did have a problem. It was not in holding false teachers at arm's length, but in tending to become lax, to "drift with the tide," as it were, and this made them an easy target for false teachers. In this way, their weakness was, in a way, connected to their strength. They approached matters somewhat lackadaisically when times were fairly good, but when times became bad, they seemed to be able to stand up for the truth.

At certain times, their devotion to God's way left a lot to be desired. Just before the apostle John died in about AD 100, this was very much the case, and he really had to rouse them to get them back. From what we know from church history, by this time the membership of the true church was small and concentrated mostly around John in the church at Ephesus and some of the nearby towns in Asia Minor that he directly pastored.

Jude recognized the beginning of this drifting when he wrote in the mid-60s. All the apostles wrote similar things in their epistles: that the members of the church needed to get on the stick because false doctrines and false teachers were already in evidence among them and beginning to cause problems. If they did not root them out quickly, destruction would follow. The brethren were far too tolerant of divergent beliefs and practices, and Jude, especially, makes this point rather bluntly. He basically yells at them. Those who know Greek intimately say his language is very terse and sharp, and with it he lays in to them for being too tolerant of untruth.

His brother, Jesus, is more circumspect in His wording:

(**Revelation 2:5**) *"Remember therefore from whence thou art fallen, and repent, and do the first works; or else I will come unto thee quickly, and will remove thy candlestick out of his place, except thou repent."*

To paraphrase, he says, "I would rather that you were strong all the time. You need to go back and do the first works and remain strong so that these false teachers do not get a foothold in the church in the first place."

(**Revelation 2:14-15**) *"But I have a few things against thee, because thou hast there them that hold the doctrine of Balaam, who taught Balac to cast a stumbling block before the children of Israel, to eat things sacrificed unto idols, and to commit fornication. So hast thou also them that hold the doctrine of the Nicolaitans, which thing I hate."*

The structure of this paragraph ties together the doctrine of Balaam, the sins of eating things sacrificed to idols and committing sexual immorality, and the doctrine of the Nicolaitans. Christ implies that all three are the same basic heresy under different guises. This antinomian teaching affected the church in Thyatira as well.

Moses records Balaam's story in (**Numbers 22-25-31**). Balak, king of Moab, hires Balaam to curse the Israelites, but every time he tries, Balaam instead blesses them. He then counsels Balak to send Moabite a Midianite women into the camp of Israel to seduce the men and invite them to the sacrifices of their god (**Numbers 25:1-2; 31:16**). Clearly, Balaam's instruction included getting the Israelites to commit idolatry and sexual immorality.

Interestingly, these two practices arise in the Jerusalem Council in AD 49. Paul and Barnabas, with Peter's help, convince the assembled elders that Gentile converts to Christianity should not be required to be circumcised and keep the law of Moses, Judaism's rigorous "yoke" of picayune laws (**Acts 15:10**). However, the Council enjoins the Gentiles on four points of typical Gentile religious practice:

(**Acts 15:28-29**) *"For it seemed good to the Holy Spirit, and to us, to lay upon you no greater burden than these necessary things: that ye abstain from meats offered to idols, from blood, from things strangled, and from things fornication: from which if ye keep yourselves, ye shall do well. Fare ye well."*

Obviously, the Council's decree does not exempt Gentiles from keeping the Ten Commandments, for it is clear from many New Testament passages that Jesus and the apostles taught them to both Jews and Gentiles c.f. (**Matthew 19:17-19; Romans 13:9**) are but a few. These two issues - idolatry and sexual immorality - became a flashpoint in the conflict between true Christianity and Hellenistic Gnosticism, and a person's stance on them exposed which side he favored. Thus, Nicolaitanism and Balaamism are biblical symbols or representatives of the larger Gnostic, antinomian influence on Christianity.

Is Nicolaitanism passé? Evidently not, for Jesus' admonitions in Revelation 2 indicate that this antinomian influence will remain until His return. Notice His warnings to Pergamos and Thyatira:

(**Revelation 2: 16**) *"Repent, or else I will come unto thee quickly, and will fight against them with the sword of My mouth."*

(**Revelation 2:24-25**) *"But unto you I say, and to the rest in Thyatira, as many as have not this doctrine, and which have not known the depths of Satan, [another* allusion to antinomianism*], as they speak; I will put upon you no other burden. But that which ye have already hold fast till I come."*

This does not mean that the particular sins of eating meat sacrificed to idols and sexual license will pervade the church until the end, although idolatry and sexual sins will certainly exist in it. (And if you take a look around you, you can see that they do.) He is more concerned about the antinomian spirit, the attitude of lawlessness that allows these sins to infest the church. When members of the church teach and practice that they are not obliged to keep the laws of God, sin will inevitably break out vigorously. When this occurs, Christians are no longer under grace but under the penalty of the law and the wrath of the Judge see (**Romans 6:11-23; Hebrews 10:26-31; 12:25**).

Jesus, Paul, Peter, Jude, and John warn against the encroachment of antinomianism or lawlessness. In His Olivet Prophecy, Jesus says:

(**Matthew 24:11-12**) "*And many false prophets shall rise, and deceive many. And because iniquity shall abound, the love of many shall wax cold.*"

What will happen to such lawless people? Jesus Himself answers:

(**Matthew 7:22-23**) "*Many will say to Me in that day, "Lord, Lord, have we not prophesied in thy name? And in thy name have cast out devils? And in thy name, and done many wonderful works? And then will I profess unto them, "I never knew you; depart from Me, ye that work iniquity.*"

Among Paul's end-time prophecies is his prediction of a great apostasy that results from the unrestrained assault of "*the mystery of lawlessness*" (**2 Thessalonians 2:1-7**). This comes with all unrighteous deception among those who perish, because they did not receive the love of the truth, that they might be saved. And for this reason God will send them strong delusion that they should believe the lie that they all may be condemned who did not believe the truth but had pleasure in unrighteousness. Therefore, brethren, stand fast and hold the traditions which you were taught.

Peter and Jude use similar language in their books to counter the antinomian teaching extant in their congregations. C.f. (**2 Peter 2:9-10, 12-13, 15, 18-19; 3:17-18; Jude 3-4**) John's epistles are likewise full of warnings against antinomian heresies. For instance, notice these passages:

(**1 John 2:3-4**) "*And hereby we do know that we know him, if we keep his commandments. He that saith, I know him, and keepth not his commandments, is a liar, and the truth is not in him.*"

(**1 John 3:4**) "*Whosoever committeth sin transgresseth also the law: for sin is the transgression of the law.*"
(**1 John 3:10**) "*In this the children of God are manifest, and the children of the devil: whosoever doeth not righteousness is not of God, neither he that loveth not his brother.*"

(1 **John 5:2-3**) *"By this we know that we love the children of God, when we love God, and keep his commandments. For this is the love of God, that we keep his commandments: and his commandments are not grievous."*

(2 **John 1:9-11**) *"Whosoever transgresseth, and abideth not in the doctrine of Christ, hath not God. He that abideth in the doctrine of Christ, he hath both the Father and the Son. If there come any unto you, and bring not this doctrine, receive him not into your house, neither bid him God speed: For he that biddeth him God speed is partaker of his evil deeds."*

(3 **John 1:11**) *"Beloved, follow not that which is evil, but that which is good. He that doeth good is of God: but he that doeth evil hath not seen God."*

In addition, the gospel of John uses Jesus' own words during His ministry to attack antinomian heresies in the church. This much scriptural attention along with its prophetic implications warrants our taking careful notice.

For a more detailed look at God's Ten Commandments see my book (God' said).

7 ISLAM THE NEW THREAT

Apostasy on the rise in Europe

Let's start with a fairly universal understanding of the term "apostasy" or falling away, by reviewing what's going on in Europe, from Soeren Kern at the Gatestone Institute, with "Muslims Converting Empty European Churches into Mosques":

Muslims in Europe are increasingly converting empty Christian churches into mosques.

The proliferation of mosques housed in former churches reflects the rise of Islam as the fastest growing religion in a post-Christian Europe."

As Islam replaces Christianity as the dominant religion in Europe, more and more churches are set to become mosques, which increasingly serve not only as religious institutions but also function as the foundational political building blocks for the establishment of separate, parallel Muslim communities in Europe that are based on Islamic Sharia law. (Already Sharia law is practiced in much of Europe.)

In addition to Roman Catholic churches, some Protestant churches have also been converted into mosques in Germany, where the Muslim population has jumped from around 50,000 in the early 1980s to more than 4 million today.

In Germany as a whole, more than 400 Roman Catholic churches and more than 100 Protestant churches have been closed since 2000, according to one estimate. Another 700 Roman Catholic churches are slated to be closed over the next several years.

Overall, at least 10,000 churches have been closed in Britain since 1960, including 8,000 Methodist churches and 1,700 Anglican churches. Another 4,000 churches are set to be closed by 2020, according to Christian Research, an organization that tracks religious trends in Britain.

By contrast, there are now more than 1,700 official mosques in Britain, many converted from former churches.

Many more insights from the other side of the pond can even be appreciated by agnostics or atheists, who don't welcome the prospect of their heirs being subjugated to Muhammad's followers under Islamic Sharia law, any more than any other non-Muslims would.

When a Jewish newspaper has to point it out, which says a lot? "Europe's Supersessionism: Islam Replaces Christianity:" "The new "replacement" is not the old anti-Semitic theory but an anti-Christian fact. As the churches disappear, it is hard not to think of how these same Christians burned Jewish synagogues."

It certainly wouldn't be the first time that God used some of His enemies, in judgment against some of His people, for losing their love of truth.

Pope Francis seems headed on a course intended to redefine Roman Catholic Church doctrine to confirm it to the world as well.

(**2 Thessalonians 2:3-4**) *"Let no man deceive you by any means: for [that day shall not come], except there come a falling away first, and that man of sin be revealed, the son of perdition; Who opposeth and exalteth himself above all that is called God, or that is worshipped; so that he as God sitteth in the temple of God."*

Has "that man of sin" been revealed during this "falling away"? Where is the "temple of God" ever since Jesus raised it up in three days, just as He indicated that He could? The temple of God is the corporate body of Christ! It's the "church".

Religious Pluralism

Few groups seem to be working harder, at building one-way bridges away from Jesus in surrender to Islam, than the group that may well be the largest that calls itself "A Common Word between Us and You". As if there could be common ground between Christianity and the specifically "antichrist, counter-gospel, hate-filled, anti-religion of Islam."

A Common Word will likely pose the greatest danger to free speech regarding Muhammad and his following as revealed through Islam's own books, and advancement of the agenda of orthodox Muslims that are responsible for well over 70% of the murder, mayhem and misery being visited upon the civilized world. Of course the Muhammadans will take from the organization what they want, which is to silence the Gospel of Jesus Christ, while the Ivy League left wing University styled self-described "Christians" will need to remain silent regarding the crucifixion of Christ and the saving grace of His shed blood or confessing that Jesus is the Son of God, so as to avoid "offending" their Muslim now-masters.

Even a child can see that the only dialogue that should be taking place between the western styled peaceful heterodox Muslim "hypocrites", and their orthodox violent brethren in the cradle of the religion that get Islam like the Islamic scholar Abu Bakr al-Baghdadi who heads up The Islamic State, or outsiders like British Cleric Anjem Choudary. The feigning-peace apostates need to edit the Quran and Hadith until they offer no excuses and rewrite 1400 years of Islamic history, before they begin to try to sell their dissimulation/taqiyyah and absurd notion of Islam being peaceful to Christians, that have followed the Prince of Peace for 2000 years and whose Gospel needs no edit to be the very embodiment of love and roadmap to a peaceful world.

In bed with the U.N.: "A Common Word has received numerous awards, has been the basis for many resolutions and peace initiatives, and gave birth to the UN World Interfaith Harmony Week, and much more." How long will it be before they join Hillary Clinton and the OIC nations that impose the death penalty by statute for the "crime" of "blasphemy", in pushing for U.N. anti-blasphemy laws?

Based on what seems to be largely Islamic membership, perhaps it should be called something more like "Muslims engaged in dissimulation and taqiyyah to dupe the cognitively impaired wishful".

Are the non-Muslim members of this mutual apostasy club so ignorant to Islam, as to not know there can only be one-way bridges built between Islam and anyone else, since Muhammad's followers are prohibited from even making friends of Jews and Christians.

So, all Islamic leaders who come to British and American Church leaders for inter-faith co-operation are either defying the instructions of Allah or they have a hidden agenda. The Islam of the 7th century AD is the same today, probably under new guises as the situation demands. It is the same tactic of "No compulsion in religion" that Mohammed first adapted to Christians and Jews that Muslims are using in the Western world today."

There are so many incitements against Christians and non-Muslims running through the pages of the Quran that we find it hard to believe that anybody can be a real practicing Muslim now or then and not hate Christians. It is impossible. Any Muslim who is not violent (secretly or openly) is hardly a real Muslim, at least not in the Quranic sense."

Thus we find the concept of taqiyyah, or lying in the cause of "Allah", according to Sunni Muslim theologian Abu Ha-med Mohammad ibn Mohammad al-Ghazzali of the Shafi school:

Speaking is a means to achieve objectives. If a praiseworthy aim is attainable through both telling the truth and lying, it is unlawful to accomplish it through lying because there is no need for it. When it is possible to achieve such an aim by lying but not by telling the truth, it is permissible to lie if attaining the goal is permissible..., and obligatory to lie if the goal is obligatory. ...One should compare the bad consequences entailed by lying to those entailed by telling the truth, and if the consequences of telling the truth are more damaging, one is entitled to lie.

An "obligatory" "goal": "Da'wah is recognized by the majority of scholars as being obligatory upon every Muslim."

Da'wah is proselytizing for Islam, so when it is not possible to achieve this goal by telling the truth in an interfaith dialogue, Muslims are under obligation to lie while proselytizing. An example of this could be to claim there is a history of Mecca from prior to the 4th century AD when the person proselytizing knows there is absolutely no evidence whatsoever to support that lie.

Relentless Muslims murdering, persecuting, torturing Christians in Muslim countries, and the world says nothing. Note that the same silence preceded the Nazi genocide of twelve million people.

Instead, the world advances the savages' narrative that opposition to jihad and sharia is "islamophobia." Vilified are the few who dare to speak out against this vicious anti-human system of oppression. And their dissemblers in the media and proxies in the West like CAIR, ICNA, ISNA, MSA, Aslan Media, etc., are lauded and loved.

Where are the church leaders speaking out against Muslim genocide of Christians? They are busy providing cover for the annihilationist by playing patsy in the interfaith dialogue ruse."

Beyond ecumenism and even beyond religious pluralism, are "Christians" who cast their lots in with such as the "International Interfaith Council".

Add to them the interfaith pluralist wolves in sheep's clothing heretics, that are selling out Jesus to Muhammad's antichrists through the "A Common Word between Us and You", and things would seem to be accelerating even more exponentially. Imagine suggesting a "common word" when each and every Muslim is required to deny the crucifixion of Christ, and thus reject His shed blood, and deny the Son of God, as articles of their faith in the false prophet Muhammad alone. Are even taught that to confess that Jesus is the Son of God or even pray in Jesus' name, would be to commit the single most "heinous" and only unforgivable sin in Muhammad's cult.

Christian heretics that are apparently so ignorant to scripture, or are so filled with the spirit of antichrist, as to pretend there is a relationship between the one true God of the Jews and Christians named YHWH - Yahweh - as revealed through all of His prophets and witnesses, that His people have followed through two covenants for 3500 years.

And the one that is worshipped in the names of the Arabian pagan's deity "Allah" and his "messenger" Muhammad, through a stand-alone 23-

year 7th century record of the false prophet from the SW Arabian desert located 1200 kilometers away from THE Holy Land of the prophets and patriarchs, who came along over 500 years after the scriptures were closed and proclaimed the EXACT OPPOSITE of the WHOLE SUBJECT of the Gospel. His followers even prostrate themselves five times a day toward the very same black stone idol in Mecca, that the Quraish pagans venerated long before Muhammad adopted, and adapted, their pagan rituals to his new anti-religion. As an article of their faith in Muhammad alone, his followers are even obligated to travel to that black stone idol in Mecca, march around it and kiss it or point to it on each time around, while engaging in thinly veneered pagan Arabian moon, sun, star and jinn-devil worship rituals, as the Arabian pagans did on their pilgrimages before Muhammad was ever born.

As Christians we are to love the followers of the false prophet Muhammad so much that we are desperate to help them find their way to the foot of the cross. Invite them into our churches to learn about the love of the one true God of the scriptures as expressed through our Lord and Savior Jesus Christ. To proclaim that Jesus Christ died for us all, so we don't have to die a second death from our sins. But from Radical Islam we find antichrist Imams are advancing Islamic blasphemy from right within the evermore pluralistic "church."

The Muslim Public Affairs Council's choice of location for its 12th Annual Convention on December 15 is telling: The All Saints Episcopal Church of Pasadena, California. The group, founded by Muslim Brotherhood followers, says this is the "next step in its mission by crossing the interfaith line."

Yet again, the Islamists are taking advantage of naïve Christians with a desire to show off their tolerance.

The All Saints Episcopal Church of Pasadena started an Interfaith Study Group in 2007 with the Pasadena Jewish Temple and the Islamic Center of Southern California (ICSC), from which MPAC originated. The organization was founded as a branch of ICSC in 1986 and then became independent in 1988, though the two remain intertwined."

The ICSC is proud of its interfaith successes. For example, the First United Methodist Church of Santa Monica is allowing the ICSC to hold Friday prayers there every week.

Front Page Magazine excerpts: "Last month, a new mosque called the ICNA (Islamic Circle of North America) Islamic Center opened in Alexandria, Virginia. ICNA, an Islamist group with origins in the Jamaat-e-Islami of Pakistan, framed its inauguration as an interfaith victory, giving thanks to the three churches that let them worship on their premises as the mosque project was completed.

The two-story mosque replaced a house that was bought by ICNA in

2000. It says the facility cost $850,000 to build and can accommodate about 150 people. Good Shepherd Catholic Church, St. Luke's Episcopal Church and Aldersgate United Methodist Church allowed ICNA's Northern Virginia chapter to worship as the mosque was being built.

A 1991 U.S. Muslim Brotherhood strategic memorandum, which says its "work in America is a kind of grand jihad in eliminating and destroying the Western civilization from within," lists ICNA as one of "our organizations and the organizations of our friends." The memo refers to productive meetings between ICNA and the U.S. Muslim Brotherhood "in an attempt to reach a unity of merger." ICNA has long held its annual conferences in conjunction with the Muslim American Society, an arm of the Muslim Brotherhood, in apparent fulfillment of this objective."

From Wikipedia on the Presbyterian Church (not all of which are partial-preterist/anti-Zionist/punitive-supersessionists, as part of this denomination are futurists)

Ronald H. Stone, John Witherspoon Professor of Christian Ethics at Pittsburgh Theological Seminary, attracted negative media attention during the tour after being quoted as saying, "We treasure the precious words of Hezbollah and your expression of goodwill toward the American people. Also we praise your initiative for dialogue and mutual understanding. We cherish these statements that bring us closer to you. As an elder of our church, I'd like to say that according to my recent experience, relations and conversations with Islamic leaders are a lot easier than dealings and dialogue with Jewish leaders."

Driven by punitive Supersessionism they laud praises on an internationally recognized Islamic terrorist organization while distancing themselves from Israeli Jews. The context suggests they were likely as much fooled by Islamic terrorist's taqiyyah and subterfuge, as their doctrine made them unable to face the truth, as expressed by Jewish leaders.

Chrismal

The liberal ecumenical church is increasingly given over to religious pluralism, through such as the "Chrismal" movement, which seeks to replace truth with "tolerance". As if Jesus sat down at the tables with the moneychangers and offered to help them count their change, before politely but apologetically and gently suggesting to them, that there was a possibility that their being there may perhaps not be the best thing - though the ecumenical church doesn't even seem to go that far.

The Presbyterian Church, among the leading anti-Zionist institutions, that is working feverishly toward advancing the Islamic conquest of Israel. From their "Israel and Palestine General Assembly Action".

It calls on the General Assembly to oppose Christian Zionism and to develop a plan to communicate the theological and political ramifications it engenders to the Presbyterian Church (U.S.A.), in the mass media, and among U.S. government officials."

Chrismal Starts To Spread In America

The Rev. Rick Warren, pastor of Saddleback Church in Lake Forest and one of America's most influential Christian leaders, has embarked on an effort to heal divisions between evangelical Christians and Muslims by partnering with Southern California mosques and proposing a set of theological principles that includes acknowledging that Christians and Muslims worship the same God however nothing could be further from the truth.

The effort, informally dubbed King's Way, caps years of outreach between Warren and Muslims. Warren has broken Ramadan fasts at a Mission Viejo mosque; He has even met Muslim leaders abroad and addressed 8,000 Muslims at a national convention in Washington D.C.

The efforts by a prominent Christian leader to bridge what polls show is a deep rift between Muslims and evangelical Christians culminated in December at a dinner at Saddleback attended by 300 Muslims and members of Saddleback's congregation.

At the dinner, Abraham Meulenberg, a Saddleback pastor in charge of interfaith outreach, and Jihad Turk, director of religious affairs at a mosque in Los Angeles, introduced King's Way as "a path to end the 1,400 years of misunderstanding between Muslims and Christians."

Have you ever read anything so absurd as a Christian characterizing 1,400 years of Islamic conquest, terrorism, murder, and subjugation of Christians and Jews to the slavery of dhimmitude, as "misunderstanding between Muslims and Christians"? Let alone that Christian's understanding that the false Muhammad's stand-alone antichrist 7th century antichrist anti-religion, professes the exact opposite of the whole subject of the Gospel, to be "1,400 years of misunderstanding"? As if Warren's 21st century pop-counter-Gospel religious pluralism somehow constitutes understanding? Not even realizing he is being drawn down a one-way street through taqiyyah, while at the same time encouraging those poor sorely deluded followers of Muhammad alone, to remain on the path they are on.

(**John 3:36**) *"He that believeth on the Son hath everlasting life: and he that believeth not the Son shall not see life; but the wrath of God abideth on him."*

(**1 John 2:22**) *"Who is a liar but he that denieth that Jesus is the Christ? He is antichrist that denieth the Father and the Son. Whosoever denieth the Son, the same hath not the Father.*

Rick Warren who is one of Barak Obama's bridges to the evangelical church, he managed to pray an inaugural prayer that made nearly everyone happy, with the exception, that is, of the one true God to whom the prayer was supposed to be addressed. While Warren began by quoting the Hebrew Schema, and addressing the biblical God of all creation, who warned, *"You shall have no other gods before Me....for I, the LORD your God, am a jealous God..."* (**Exodus 20:3, 5**), Warren went on to invoke the Muslim deity Allah. If that was not bad enough, Warren quoted both the Bible and the Koran, and he prayed in the names of Jesus Christ as well as the Muslim prophet Isa! I felt this perilous travesty needed to be addressed, especially since Time Magazine has dubbed Rick Warren "America's New People's Pastor," and he is influencing millions of people through his books and public persona.

Tragically, Warren's incorporation of the Islamic deity in the name of a Muslim prophet went over the heads of the vast majority of Christians who heard his inaugural prayer. While Warren's prayer may have pleased President Barack Obama, who gained countless votes by riding on Warren's back into the evangelical church, God warned us in His Word that religious syncretism would characterize the great apostasy of the last days see (**Revelation 17**)!

While I suspected that Warren's prayer would be as inclusive as possible, even I was surprised when Warren actually quoted the Koran and used the oft-repeated Koranic formulation for Allah i.e., 'The compassionate and merciful one.' In fact, of the 114 chapters in the Koran, 113 of them begin by describing Allah as 'The compassionate and merciful one.'"

The etymology of the name "Allah" suggesting it was the proper name of the Arabian pagan's moon god. It will NEVER be the name of the one true God of the scriptures' YHWH as it occurs nearly 7,000 times in scripture and in paleo-Hebrew inscription that dates to the 9th century AD.

As if we worship the same God when Muslims prostrate themselves toward the Quraish pagan's black stone idol in Mecca, while praying in the "vain repetitions of the heathen", in the names of the Arabian pagan's deity "Allah" and his "messenger" Muhammad. Muslims commit the most egregious and only unforgivable sin according to Muhammad, if they were to confess that Jesus is the Son of God, or even pray in Jesus' name.

(**1 John 4:15**) *"Whosoever shall confess that Jesus is the Son of God, God dwelleth in him, and he in God."*

Continuing from the first Chrislam article: "'I don't know if you have noticed this, but God likes variety,' Warren told an audience of 8,000 Muslims at a Washington, D.C. convention in 2009"

"'He calls me his Muslim brother,' Barakat said. 'It all started with a friendship.'"

Is Rick Warren not aware that true Muslims aren't allowed to make friends with Christians and Jews, except to create the appearance thereof for an advantage toward dawah (proselytizing), by engaging in "taqiyyah" or Islamic subterfuge?

Can we suppose Christians will be invited into mosques to witness to Muslims on the crucifixion and shed blood of the Lamb of God to our "Muslim brothers"? That is, the whole subject of the Gospel, and indeed of the whole bible and after all, what we are commissioned to do.

(**1 Corinthians 1:23**) *"But we preach Christ crucified, unto the Jews a stumbling block, and unto the Greeks foolishness;"*

Faith Shared asks houses of worship across the country to organize events involving clergy reading from each other's sacred texts. An example would be a Christian Minister, Jewish Rabbi and Muslim Imam participating in a worship service or other event.

Suggested readings will be provided from the Torah, the Gospels, and the Qur'an, but communities are encouraged to choose readings that will resonate with their congregations. Involvement of members from the Muslim community is key.

We will also provide suggestions on how to incorporate this program into your regular worship services. And we will assist local congregations in their media and communications efforts.

Tensions around Islam in America have erupted throughout the country in the past year, leading to misconceptions, distrust and in some cases violence. News stories on the rising tide of anti-Muslim bigotry and violence abound, with graphic and often searing images of the antagonists, the protagonists and the battlegrounds where they meet. All too often, media coverage simplistically pits Muslims against would-be Qur'an burners, neglecting any substantive representation of where the majority of Americans actually stand: a shared commitment to tolerance and freedom. We are committed to ensuring that the storyline changes dramatically in 2011 by helping to create an environment of mutual understanding and respect for each other's faith traditions."

Typical liberal liars continue to persist in painting Christians - that are at least Christian enough to recognize the 1400 year reign of antichrist Islamic evil and murder of God's people and that Muhammad proclaimed the exact opposite of the whole subject of the Gospel - as harboring "anti-Muslim bigotry". However it is always in fact solely about being against Muhammad's blasphemy and not about being anti-Muslim, though liberal liars always try to pretend that being against the anti-religion of Islam, is being against persons or hating Muslims. While seeking to help them overcome the false prophet Muhammad, is specifically and expression of

Christian love, for those so sorely deluded.

With over 20,000 deadly Islamic terror attacks around the world just since 9-11, during this Second Islamic Jihad in the image of the First Islamic Jihad conquest of nearly the whole known world, one would think even Warren would get the hint. That imperialistic conquest, murder and mayhem being perfectly consistent, with what Islam's books command of Muhammad's true followers, as well as describing Muhammad's own behavior. Those who would deny this in favor of false hope are peddling the only "storyline"! There's little doubt that most of those churches are partial preterits and punitive Supersessionism.

Do you suppose those Imams will be "sharing" such verses as the following marching orders from the Quran and Hadith? From one of the most consummate and self-admitted terrorists in history:

(**Sura 8:12**) "I will instill terror into the hearts of the unbelievers: smite ye above their necks and smite all their finger-tips off them"

(**John 16:2**) *"They shall put you out of the synagogues: yea, the time cometh, that whosoever killeth you will think that he doeth God service."*

Bukhari, Narrated Ibn 'Umar: Allah's Apostle said: "I have been ordered (by Allah) to fight against the people until they testify that none has the right to be worshipped but Allah and that Muhammad is Allah's Apostle, and offer the prayers perfectly and give the obligatory charity, so if they perform that, then they save their lives as property from me except for Islamic laws and then their reckoning (accounts) will be done by Allah."

The best among the people is that believer who strives his utmost in Allah's Cause with both his life and property.

Al-Jihad (the holy fighting) in Allah's Cause (with full force of number and weaponry) is given the utmost importance in Islam and is one of its pillars (on which it stands). By Jihad Islam is established, Allah's Word is made superior, [His Word being La ilaha ill-Allah (which means: none has the right to be worshipped by Allah] and His Religion (Islam) is propagated. By abandoning Jihad (may Allah protect us from that) Islam is destroyed and the Muslims fall into an inferior position; there honor is lost, their lands are stolen, their rule and authority vanish. Jihad is an obligatory duty in Islam on every Muslim, and he who tries to escape from this duty, or does not in his innermost heart wish to fulfill this duty, dies with one of the qualities of a hypocrite.

Of course, nobody can offer Salat, prayer and observe Saum, fast, incessantly, and since the Muslim fighter is rewarded as if he was doing subh good impossible deeds, no possible deed equals Jihad in reward.

The Roman Catholic Church on Islam

The Church regards with esteem also the Moslems. They adore the one God, living and subsisting in Himself, merciful and all-powerful, the Creator of heaven and earth, who has spoken to men; they take pains to submit wholeheartedly to even His inscrutable decrees, just as Abraham, with whom the faith of Islam takes great pleasure in linking itself, submitted to God. Though they do not acknowledge Jesus as God, they revere Him as a prophet. They also honor Mary, His virgin mother; at times they even call on her with devotion. In addition, they await the Day of Judgment when God will render their deserts to all those who have been raised up from the dead. Finally, they value the moral life and worship God especially through prayer, almsgiving and fasting.

Since in the course of centuries not a few quarrels and hostilities have arisen between Christians and Moslems, this Sacred Synod urges all to forget the past and to work sincerely for mutual understanding and to preserve as well as to promote together for the benefit of all mankind social justice and moral welfare, as well as peace and freedom."

It seems the Roman Church fell into the common error of believing that simply because Muhammad's followers proclaim they "believe in Jesus", that somehow means that they do, even though Muhammad proclaimed the exact opposite of the whole subject of the Gospel. Thus 1.5 billion people in the world today, must reject the shed blood of the Lamb of God, as an article of their faith in Muhammad alone. Are Roman Catholics to imagine that the Pope and Vatican Council were somehow just ignorant to that fact when assembling "infallible" doctrine?

Let's consider their statement part by part, since what the Pope and Vatican Council proclaim, are what Roman Catholics are compelled to believe.

"The Church regards with esteem also the Moslems. They adore the one God,"

Muhammad's followers worship in the names of a pagan Arabian deity "Allah" and his "messenger" Muhammad. The name of the "one God" is YHWH as occurs nearly 7,000 times in scripture and in pale-Hebrew inscription discovered that date as early as the 9th century BC. That is the name of the God of the scriptures, regardless of the name that misguided Arabic speaking Christians and Jews assign Him. Indeed the Arabic language didn't even exist until a few centuries into the Christian era. Additionally, a Muslim would be committing the only unforgivable sin according to Muhammad, if he were to even pray in Jesus name.

Living and subsisting in Himself; merciful and all- powerful, the Creator of heaven and earth, who has spoken to men."

Indeed He has, so let's hear Him:

(**Matthew 3:17**) "*And lo a voice from heaven, saying, this is my beloved Son, in whom I am well pleased.*"

(**Mark 1:11**) "*And there came a voice from heaven, [saying], Thou art my beloved Son, in whom I am well pleased.*"

(**Luke 3:22**) "*And a voice came from heaven, which said, Thou art my beloved Son; in thee I am well pleased.*"

(**2 Peter 1:17**) "*For he received from God the Father honor and glory, when there came such a voice to him from the excellent glory, this is my beloved Son, in whom I am well pleased.*"

They take pains to submit wholeheartedly to even His inscrutable decrees.

Perhaps by prostrating toward the Quraish pagan's black stone idol in Mecca five times a day? Let alone Muhammad ordering up his "Allah's" curse on God's people, like some sort of a voodoo incantation, for being "deluded away from the Truth.

(**1 John 2:22-23**) "*Who is a liar but he that denieth that Jesus is the Christ? He is antichrist that denieth the Father and the Son. Whosoever denieth the Son, the same hath not the Father.*"

Just as Abraham, with whom the faith of Islam takes pleasure in linking itself, submitted to God.

Abraham smashed all of his father's idols while Mohammedans venerate the Quraish pagan's black stone idol. They are unwittingly "submitted" to Satan through the spirit of antichrist. The only anti-a-specific-religion, cult on earth. Recitations conspicuously co-authored by the jealous opposer of Jesus Christ, who transformed himself into an angel of light, to his prophet Mohammed.

(**2 Corinthians 11:14**) "*And no marvel; for Satan himself is transformed into an angel of light.*'"

Muhammad didn't even don the "sheep's clothing" but came conquering as a "ravening wolf".

(**Matthew 7:15**) "*Beware of false prophets, which come to you in sheep's clothing, but inwardly they are ravening wolves.*"

Even without the sheep's clothing he apparently still fooled the Roman

Church.....

(**Mark 13:22**) *"For false Christ's and false prophets shall rise, and shall shew signs and wonders, to seduce, if [it were] possible, even the elect."*

But there are some of us that Mohammed didn't fool. Indeed even Mohammed believed it was a jinn-demon that first met him in that cave, until his wife Khadijah and her cousin talked him out of it.

Though they do not acknowledge Jesus as God .

They deny the deity of Christ along with denying His crucifixion, death and resurrection, while denying that Jesus is the Son of God. But hey, why trifle in minor details eigh?

Again, the most egregious and only unforgivable sin according to Muhammad ("shirk"), would be committed if a Muslim were to confess that Jesus is the Son of God, or even to pray in Jesus' name. A sin worse than child rape or cold blooded mass murder.

(**1 John 4:15**) *"Whosoever shall confess that Jesus is the Son of God, God dwelleth in him, and he in God."*

(**1 John 5:12**) *"He that hath the Son hath life; [and] he that hath not the Son of God hath not life."*

They revere Him as a prophet. Which is another exactly opposite delusion they suffer because, they must reject Jesus prophecies of his own crucifixion, death and resurrection, to follow Muhammad alone. Rejecting the very blood of the Lamb of God that would save them:

(**Matthew 20:17-19**) *"And Jesus going up to Jerusalem took the twelve disciples apart in the way, and said unto them, Behold, we go up to Jerusalem; and the Son of man shall be betrayed unto the chief priests and unto the scribes, and they shall condemn him to death, And shall deliver him to the Gentiles to mock, and to scourge, and to crucify [him]: and the third day he shall rise again."*

(**Hebrews 10:29**) *"Of how much sorer punishment, suppose ye, shall he be thought worthy, who hath trodden underfoot the Son of God, and hath counted the blood of the covenant, wherewith he was sanctified, an unholy thing, and hath done despite unto the Spirit of grace?"*

They also honor Mary, His virgin Mother; at times they even call on her with devotion.

Muslims even join the Roman Catholics in the veneration of Mary at Our Lady of Fatima. Roman Catholic Mariology arriving through a series of invention and proclamation, with some declared dogma as recently as 1950.

In addition, they await the Day of Judgment when God will render their deserts to all those who have been raised up from the dead.

Are the antichrists who follow the false prophet Mohammed awaiting "that blessed hope" of Christians, or a very different day?

(**Titus 2:13**) *"Looking for that blessed hope, and the glorious appearing of the great God and our Saviour Jesus Christ;"*

Bukhari , Hadith Narrated Abu Huraira: Allah's Apostle said, "By Him in Whose Hands my soul is, son of Mary (Jesus) will shortly descend amongst you people (Muslims) as a just ruler and will break the cross and kill the pig and abolish the Jizya (a tax taken from the non-Muslims, who are in the protection, of the Muslim government). Then there will be abundance of money and no-body will accept charitable gifts.

Those poor deluded souls encouraged to remain on Muhammad's antichrist, anti-Gospel, anti-Christian and anti-Jew path, in part thanks to the Pope and Vatican Council.

(**John 3:36**) *"He that believeth on the Son hath everlasting life: and he that believeth not the Son shall not see life; but the wrath of God abideth on him."*

(**Revelation 20:10**) *"And the devil that deceived them was cast into the lake of fire and brimstone, where the beast and the false prophet [are], and shall be tormented day and night forever and ever."*

Finally, they value the moral life and worship God especially through prayer .

From "Infidel" Hirsi Ali explains part of "salat", "You say Praise be to Allah thirty-three times; God forgive me thirty-three times; Allah is great thirty-three times; and then, if you choose, you may also say Gratitude to Allah." Muslims are commanded to perform salat fives times a day, totaling 495 repetitions per day. Muhammad lifted the five required occurrences from the 2nd century occult cult of the Sabians.

Here's how scripture describes such prayer:

(**Matthew 6:7**) *"But when ye pray, use not vain repetitions, as the heathen [do]: for they think that they shall be heard for their much speaking."*

Almsgiving

Generally benefiting only the Muslim community, where were even a little bit of the trillions of dollars of oil wealth of Islamic countries, coming to the aid of even the tsunami victims of Indonesia, that has the highest Muslim population of any country on earth including 88% of Indonesians?

Fasting

Essentially skipping lunch for a month, which only helps to add to their self-delusion of self-righteousness. Indeed Muslims spend more on food during the month of Ramadan in which they "fast", than they do in any other month of the year, from feasting on extra special fare before dawn and after sunset. Many actually gain weight during the month they "fast". Besides which, Ramadan itself, is another ritual that was lifted from pagan moon worshippers.

Since the course of centuries not a few quarrels and hostilities have arisen between Christians and Moslems.

Certainly Muslims conquered Christians and nearly the whole known world, during the First Islamic Jihad, and subjugated Jews and Christians to a state of Dhimmitude. The "Christian" to Islam "hostilities" were between the Roman Catholic Church and the Moslems. But then the RCC also slaughtered Jews and Christians.

(**John 13:35**) *"By this shall all [men] know that ye are my disciples, if ye have love one to another."*

(**Galatians 5:14**) *"For all the law is fulfilled in one word, [even] in this; Thou shalt love thy neighbor as thyself."*

(**Matthew 5:44**) *"But I say unto you, Love your enemies, bless them that curse you, do good to them that hate you, and pray for them which despitefully use you, and persecute you;"*

The Crusades, inquisitions and persecution and slaughter of Muslims, Jews and Christians, were akin to the 1400 year history of murder, rape, pillage and plunder of Islamic jihad. With over 20,000 deadly Islamic terror attacks, around the world, just since 9-11. No surprise that Moslems (and agnostics as well) have a difficult time discerning a difference between historical Roman Church style "Christianity" and Islam. Read Fox's Book of the Martyrs and Martyr's Mirror they are available free online.

This sacred synod urges all to forget the past and to work sincerely for mutual understanding.

Mutual understanding in regard to our respective beliefs is impossible for a Christian, because Mohammed was as opposite to Jesus Christ, as his antichrist recitations are the opposite of the Gospel. Mutual understanding is impossible for those that are commanded to conquer and subjugate all people on earth to Muhammad's followers.

Of course a lie regarding the Gospel, but fighting and slaying non-Muslims is "a promise binding" on all true, male, followers of Muhammad.

Tabari /Ishaq the Jews were made to come down, and Allah's Messenger imprisoned them. Then the Prophet went out into the marketplace of Medina (it is still its marketplace today), and he had trenches dug in it. He sent for the Jewish men and had them beheaded in those trenches. They were brought out to him in batches. They numbered 800 to 900 boys and men.

Bukhari I entered the Mosque, saw Abu, sat beside him and asked about sex. Abu Said said, "We went out with Allah's Apostle and we received female slaves from among the captives. We desired women and we loved to do coitus interrupt us."

The difference between a Christian martyr and so-called Muslim martyr being that the Christian martyr says "I will die for what I believe in." while the Muslim so-called martyr that dies inadvertently during an act of imperialistic aggression says "You will die for what I believe in."

Perhaps the Pope and Vatican Council feel more of a kinship to Islam because of their mutual persecution of Jews that result from replacement theology, or "punitive Supersessionism".

Sahih Bukhari Narrated Abu Huraira: Allah's Apostle said, "the Hour will not be established until you fight with the Jews, and the stone behind which a Jew will be hiding will say."O Muslim! There is a Jew hiding behind me, so kill him."

And to preserve as well as to promote together for the benefit of all mankind social justice and moral welfare, as well as peace and freedom."

Freedom, liberty, self-determination, democracy and self-rule are the very antithesis of Islam, and Islamic Sharia Law. "Peace" in Islam can only be defined as a 100% Islamic state, or the "dar al Salaam" (house of peace). If you are a non-Muslim you are in the "dar al Harb" (house of war) and though you may not be at war against Islam, Islam has been at war against you for 1400 years. Islam can only survive in an oppressive, dictatorial, totalitarian state. "Social justice" is female childhood genital mutilation, chopping hands off of thieves and beheading Islamic "apostates" for coming to Christ. Locking wives in houses all day and divorcing wives by text messaging "I divorce you" three times. "Moral welfare" demonstrated in parents murdering their own children for coming to Christ, or for being a victim of rape, to preserve the family's "honor". Women having the voice of one-half that of a man in court, and receiving the same allocation of inheritance, compared to male siblings. Moral like sharia law:

Honoring women

(**John 3:16**) *"For God so loved the world that he gave his only begotten Son, that whosoever believeth in him should not perish, but have everlasting life."*

What the Pope and Vatican Council have done is encourage Muhammad's followers to continue on their antichrist path. How many millions of Muslims might have overcome Muhammad, if instead of cowering in cowardly submission to Muhammad's followers, the Pope had taken advantage of his bully pulpit to announce to the world that Muhammad proclaimed the exact opposite of the whole subject of the Gospel? If he had stood up for Jesus instead. Could it have ignited a global dialogue, and perhaps even a heated debate between Islamic leaders and their followers, and ultimately resulted in the collapse of Islam? But that would be underestimating the power of the spirit of antichrist, and also be contrary to any prophesies regarding the false prophet Muhammad and his Islamic kingdom "beast" as the final foe of God's people, let alone contrary to this prophesied apostasy as revealed only in small part on this page.

Meanwhile rather than sitting around a campfire singing kumbaya while deceptively pretending that the scriptures sanction THE false prophet Muhammad - that came along 500 years after the scriptures were closed. Christians should do everything they can to continue to help guide Muhammad's sorely deluded followers to the foot of the cross.

(**1 Corinthians 1:23**) *"But we preach Christ crucified, unto the Jews a stumbling block, and unto the Greeks foolishness;"*

(**1 Corinthians 11:4**) *"Every man praying or prophesying, having [his] head covered, dishonoureth his head."*

Perhaps the blindness of the Pope and Vatican Council is because the Roman Church shares so many parallels with Islam.

(**2 Thessalonians 2:5-12**) *"Remember ye not, that, when I was yet with you, I told you these things? And now ye know what whitholdeth that he might be revealed in his time. For the mystery of iniquity doth already work: only he who now letteth [will let], until he be taken out of the way. And then shall that Wicked be revealed, whom the Lord shall consume with the spirit of his mouth, and shall destroy with the brightness of his coming: Even him, whose coming is after the working of Satan with all power and signs and lying wonders, And with all deceivableness of unrighteousness in them that perish; because they received not the love of the truth, that they might be saved. And for this cause God shall send them strong delusion, that they should believe a lie: That they all might be damned who believed not the truth, but had pleasure in unrighteousness."*

Cults

It isn't like we weren't warned:

(**2 Timothy 4:3-4**) *"For the time will come when they will not endure sound doctrine; but after their own lusts shall they heap to themselves teachers, having itching ears; And they shall turn away [their] ears from the truth, and shall be turned unto fables."*

Some suggest that the Roman Church held a preterits view historically, but if that were the case then why would Jesuit Alcazar have needed to pen his 17th century counter-reformation invention, just a few decades after Jesuit Ribera penned his futurist counter-reformation eschatology?

8 AN UNCOMFORTABLE TRUTH

There is another big lie abroad that is weakening the church. This doctrine claims that it is impossible for those who say that they belong to God to ever desert the faith. This Laodicean deception causes spiritual sloth and indolence. The reality is that apostasy from the faith is happening all the time. And it is happening too many who think they are okay with God. This 'falling away from the faith or apostasy would not be apostasy if it was not happening to those who claim to be and probably are of God, at least for the moment. Pagans don't apostatize! They never were at God's table. So they never were in a position to leave and desert Him!

This is an uncomfortable truth. But it is needful in these times of great deception. The great "Falling away" from the faith has been prophesied by our apostle Paul.

(**Thessalonians 2:3-4**) *"Let no man deceive you by any means: for that Day will not come, except there come a falling away first, and that man of sin be revealed, the son of perdition; Who opposeth and exalteth himself above all that is called God or that is worshiped; so that he as God sitteth in the temple of God, shewing himself that he is God."*

The possibility of apostasy, desertion of God, was clearly taught by Jesus in the parable of the sower. (**Matthew 13:1-23**) The good seed sometimes falls by the road side or the rocky soil or among thorns. This new life springs up for a season and looks good for a while. Then it is choked by the thorns and cares of this world. Or the sun comes up and being without deep roots to the waters of life it withers away. Christians and also the so-called "Christian nations" can and do fall away from the faith.

King David wrote a song warning us about the end time new world order conspiracy against the covenant of Messiah. David clearly saw the end time apostasy and the raging of the nations against the legitimate blood bought righteous rule of the returning Messiah. It is laid out for us clearly in (**Psalm 2**).

What is the cause that leads people into apostasy?

(**Deuteronomy 18: 19-22**), is the test of a prophet, and (**Deuteronomy 13:1-3**), is also the test of a prophet, except the Deuteronomy 13 test of a prophet is God's testing of the hearts of the people as to whether they love him or not. Understanding the text correctly, it seems that it was a deliberate act of God to allow a false teacher into their midst.

(**Deuteronomy 13:3**) *"Thou shalt not hearken unto the words of that prophet, or that dreamer of dreams: for the LORD your God proveth you, to know whether ye love the LORD your God with all your heart and with all your soul."*

God tested the hearts of His people as to whether they were sincere of their love towards Him, and by them going after other god's was an indication to God of their insincerity. Does not God test the hearts of His people today?

What did God do with Israel when they went into apostasy? He removed His blessing by permitting other nations to bring them into captivity. This caused them to cry out and repent. Along with seeing God deliver them out of the hands of their oppressors was His awesome power in being able to do this. Even though God was always merciful to Israel, He was not tolerant with them compromising His commandments.

Exalting Man

Whether a person demonstrates extraordinary talents or not leads us to label or categorize them in some way. If someone demonstrates extraordinary talents and depending upon our personal admiration of their talent, could lead to idolizing them. Placing someone in the position of self exaltation can lead them to believe by popularity they are of greater exceptional quality than others. This incites prideful misconceptions with the possibility of delusions of grandiose. It's the age old problem from incept mankind; Eve was lied to by the Serpent he said that her and Adam could be as god's knowing good and evil. (**Genesis 3:5**)

Prevalent in the church today is how leaders who are exalting themselves above their adherents. Jesus said, *"Neither be ye called masters: for one is your Master, even Christ. But he that is greatest among you shall be your servant. And whosoever shall exalt himself shall be abased; and he that shall humble himself shall be exalted."* (**Matthew 23:10-12**) Some leaders declare themselves progressively reaching godhood, and exercise intimidation over their flocks for not being at the place of spiritual growth where they are. This attitude of superiority is severely condemned in the New Testament. Christians are *"one body"* (**1 Corinthians 12:12**) who should love one another. Spiritual gifts are for the Christian community rather than one's individual to abuse, and should be exercised in humility rather than pride. Jesus warned His disciples to beware of the doctrine of the Pharisees and of the Sadducees. A little leaven, of men s unscriptural teachings, will eventually leaveneth the whole.

There is much abuse which goes on towards God's flock by the so called shepherds. Some of the flocks are so mesmerized by the charisma of these false teachers, even if warned; they continue to follow them unquestioningly. We are not without excuse about the possibility of false prophets. The Lord has warned us of such shepherds, and one need to withdraw from them upon realizing this. Do not be intimidated by what they might have to say if after what you have become aware of and wanting to withdraw when the eyes of your understanding become enlightened. It is your God given right and choice. Read (**Ezekiel 34** and **John 10**) for confirmation of this abuse.

In the 6000 yrs of mans existence, the nature of man has not changed. The pride he had then is identical to the pride he has now. His sinful acts then are identical to his sinful acts today. Mankind is in need of the Saviour, the Saviour God made provision for all through His Son Jesus Christ, from the time they fell into sin. God's mercy has been demonstrated all the way through the entire history of mankind, who was already providing a way out for man from his fallen state immediately after the fall.

(**Genesis 3:15**) *"And I will put enmity between thee and the woman, and between thy seed and her seed; it shall bruise thy head, and thou shalt bruise his heel."*

Latter Rain Influence

(**2 Thessalonians 2:3**) *"Let no man deceive you by any means: for that day shall not come, except there come a falling away first, and that man of sin be revealed, the son of perdition;"*

What the apostle Paul says in his letter to the Thessalonians, in (**2 Thessalonians 2**), is that a falling away is going to result, and that will cause the anti-Christ, that man of sin or the son of perdition, to be revealed. We have all been informed about the inevitable new world order, world governance of which the United Nations (UN) has been instrumental in implementing. It has not been easy for the UN to establish a political climate for world unification. Many nations have told the UN not to interfere with them, and lately, rejecting the IMF's cause for globalization knowing what the end result would afford. It is a matter of fact that globalization will result in an appointment for a global leader which the Bible calls the anti-Christ. Simultaneously, a climate is being established religiously for the unification of all the world's religions by finding common ground in each of their belief systems so that they are able to merge and agree as one.

What is this falling away the apostle Paul spoke about? A falling away from what? In Strong's Concordance, the definition of "falling away" [apostasia] means "defection from truth [apostasy]." If this means defection from truth; only the biblically believing and practicing church of Jesus Christ who has their foundation upon the Rock - the custodians of the truth - could defect from the truth; who else could? Was Paul saying that those responsible for delivering the truth at some stage in history would deliver it no longer? Paul says they will no longer love the truth, and the church is the one responsible. Ignoring what God has already given us in His Word in professing to a lost world as sufficient for salvation have turned to philosophies of men, and fables (**2 Timothy 4:1-4**). They spice up the message of the cross with what they call "new revelation knowledge" in despite as to whether it lines up with the content of Scripture or not.

The consequences for no longer loving the truth are that God gives them over to a strong delusion (**2 Thessalonians 2:10-11**). If you take the time to watch some of the videos about the Toronto blessing, the Brownsville revival, Pensacola outpouring, etc., you can note one thing the Word of God never gets read because of their pre-occupation by what the "spirit" is going to do. Prevalent in these meetings is spiritual drunkenness with pandemonium. In some video clips an attempt is made to do a reading from the Bible, but then never does. Could this be what Paul says about no longer being a love for the truth? It does seem to be that way.

One can well believe that this is the case when identifying the new wave of spirituality which has no bearing upon what the Word of God declares. To me it looks like judgment has come upon the church, resulting from a falling away from truth. This mayhem being condoned by so many is alarming, and not only is it being condoned but exercised and promoted by literally every denomination there is; the alpha course paving the way. What leads one to believe that this could be the apostasy Paul speaks about in (**2 Thessalonians 2:3**) that is going to usher in the anti-Christ, is due to the wide acceptance this new wave of spirituality is having, and which is not able to be singled out as a particular groups participation alone because of the mixture of teachings which have compounded through movements as: Pentecostal Restorations, Neo-Pentecostalism, The Latter Rain movement, The Charismatic movement, The Manifest Sons of God, The Shepherding Movement, The Positive Confession Movement, Domonionism, The Fivefold Ministry, Present Truth, and new groups arising all the time.

The movements that grew out of Pentecostalism developed new

teachings and practices which became more and more extreme as they began to flourish. Let us look at the excesses of the three dominant movements: Pentecostalism, Neo-Pentecostalism Deliverance, and The Latter Rain Movement.

1. Pentecostalism = this movement is about restoration of what is lost, however it is experience-centered, personality-centered. It's all about what you can feel not what you know are what you must do which is theologically thin and divisive.

2. Neo-Pentecostal Deliverance = this movement is also about restoration and experience centered, and personality centered as well. However it adds Sensation, and lifts people up to cult like figures. It has erroneous deliverance methods, scandalous fund-raising techniques, false faith appropriation, (such as name it and clam it). It has a preoccupation with Satan, with new revelations it even has an element of anti-intellectualism.

3. Latter Rain Movement = Much like the first two this movement is also about restoration and is experience centered, and personality centered and sensation and, lifting people up to cult like figures with erroneous deliverance methods, with it's scandalous fund-raising techniques. But it adds false faith appropriation, new restoration orientation (such as the Fivefold ministry), it has extreme spiritual disciplines, it has a new prophetic outlook, recovery of true worship, immortalization of the saint's unity of the faith (or the faithful).

The newer groups popping up are practicing all the above it's a conglomeration of teachings, teachings that were once rejected by the church. Those promoting the new teachings that were rejected by the church became independent from sound theological establishments, and professed what they believed was the "new move" God is having upon the church. Whether what they taught could be compared with classical or traditional theological doctrine made no difference, new revelation knowledge was now in.

Apostasy has always resulted to some degree or another, but in the last century as never before in church history the escalation of apostasy is evident by the many pseudo Christian movements which have sprung up as tares amongst the wheat. This apostasy shall be the result of the church no longer loving and teaching the truth. This, sadly, is already the result as men teach that new knowledge, unfounded in Scripture, as being given by God known as "revelation knowledge" for this particular time in church history for revival and growth of the church.

To say that God is giving new revelation knowledge is firstly insulting to God as though He had no clue to such a time as this ever happening and so realizes the need to give men new knowledge or understanding on how to manage today's church, and secondly, if this is the case, then, the Bible cannot be dependable any longer because those who are appointed as prophets now have the answer for the church today. We may as well re-write the Bible.

Then there is another extreme, the main stream protestant church is encouraging the consolidation of all religious affiliations together under one banner, that is, the Christian church merging together with Roman Catholicism, and of which Roman Catholicism is inviting all faiths under the same umbrella. This is them who avoid being offended if a stand for declaring Jesus the way, the truth, and the life needs to be made. Jesus Christ is an embarrassment to them, and therefore excuses adherents of false religious affiliations that their beliefs are the same as Christianity.

(**1Timothy 4:1-3**) *"Now the Spirit speaketh expressly, that in the latter times some shall depart from the faith, giving heed to seducing spirits, and doctrines of devils; Speaking lies in hypocrisy; having their conscience seared with a hot iron; Forbidding to marry, and commanding to abstain from meats, which God hath created to be received with thanksgiving of them which believe and know the truth".*

In all sincerity, men and women have gone to great lengths to try to please God. Without seeking His permission, they presume to add things to the worship of God because they are attractive and have a vague attachment to the One whom they look upon as their Savior. They think their sincerity in worship is more important than the truth.

But God thinks differently:

(**Deuteronomy 12:32**) *"What thing soever I command you, observe to it: thou shalt not add thereto nor diminish from it."*

Christmas is a festival that has been added. It is syncretism, blending a practice from paganism into the stream of Christianity. Only the revelation of God shows how He will be worshipped, and He will not be served in imitation of other gods. God's way *cannot* be "improved" by human sincerity.

(**Deuteronomy 13:1-18**) defines the law regarding apostasy. Those who led others to worship other gods or adopt the practices of the nations around them were to be stoned! Cities that fell under the sway of corrupt individuals were to be attacked, burned to the ground, and left as rubble! God considers tampering with His truth to be evil that must be eradicated!

Apostasy begins with the perverse drive in man to push beyond the bounds of what has been revealed by God as the basis for His way of life. When God gives instruction, He frequently does so in broad generalities. Within the perimeters of those broad generalities, He expects us to explore and to apply them in their spirit and intent. Unfortunately, history reveals that that has not been mankind's approach. Man has consistently tried to "improve" upon God's revelation using his limited reason and logic.

Earlier, God had informed Adam and Eve that sin exacts a penalty, death – the cessation of life – and, if a person will not repent of sin, this means total death – no chance for eternal life. This threat God has held over mankind's head from the beginning. Notice, however, how the Devil relies:

(**Genesis 3:4-5**) *"And the serpent said to the woman, "Ye will not surely die. For God doth know that in that day ye eat thereof your eyes shall be opened, and ye shall be as Gods, knowing good and evil."*

Here is the lie: "Look, Adam and Eve, you have an immortal soul. God cannot enforce his threat." In its various forms though the centuries, this doctrine of man having eternal life already has appeared time and again.

In theological terms, this belief is the basis of the "Doctrine of Eternal Security." What is worse, this heretical doctrine has resurfaced in the church, having been part of the latest apostasy. It cannot stand, however, before the light of God's Word. God has a far superior way of dealing with humanity – both righteous and incorrigible.

9 VANITY COMES BEFORE THE FALL

Moses had placed Aaron in charge while he received instruction from God on Mount Sinai. Giving him the benefit of the doubt, Aaron probably lacked the conviction or courage to fill Moses' shoes adequately in his absence. To stall for time, he asked the people to contribute to the cause, hoping to deter them. Understanding the principle of *"For where your treasure is, there your heart will be also."* (**Matthew 6:21**), he asked them to donate some of their jewelry.

His plan failed. They eagerly gave of their treasure, showing where their heart really was. Now Aaron had to go through with it, and he did.

A major motivator in the process of apostasy is contained within the words, "Moses delayed his coming." Impatience, weariness with the way, and the constant struggle without any indication of relief are all included. God repeats this in the New Testament, when Christ warns that the evil servant says, *"My master is delaying His coming"* (**Matthew 24:48; Luke 12:45**). God emphasizes it just in case His children's endurance begins to lag. He does not want anyone to turn aside to some exciting distraction in the surrounding culture.

(**Deuteronomy 13:1-5**) *"If there arise among you a prophet, or a dreamer of dreams, and giveth thee a sign or a wonder, And the sign or the wonder come to pass, whereof he spake unto thee, saying, Let us go after other gods, which thou hast not known, and let us serve them; Thou shalt not hearken unto the words of that prophet, or that dreamer of dreams: for the LORD your God proveth you, to know whether ye love the LORD your God with all your heart and with all your soul. Ye shall walk after the LORD your God, and fear him, and keep his commandments, and obey his voice, and ye shall serve him, and cleave unto him. And that prophet, or that dreamer of dreams, shall be put to death; because he hath spoken to turn you away from the LORD your God, which brought you out of the land of Egypt, and redeemed you out of the house of bondage, to* *thrust thee out of the way which the LORD thy God commanded thee to walk in. So shalt thou put the evil away from the midst of thee."*

This is the earliest formal warning to God's people that attacks against their faith would take place within the fellowship of His children, and the pattern has occurred repeatedly. God rises up a prophet or minister to instruct His people. Opposition arises, usually in the form of ministers who see things differently, who force the people to choose which way they will follow. Understand, God is not passively watching. He actively tests His children's loyalties through such calamitous situations.

God's Sovereignty and the Church's Condition

(**Joshua 7:20-21**) *"And Achan answered Joshua, and said, Indeed I have sinned against the LORD God of Israel, and thus and thus have I done: When I saw among the spoils a goodly Babylonish garment, and two hundred shekels of silver, and a wedge of gold of fifty shekels weight, then I coveted them, and took them; and, behold, they are hid in the earth in the midst of my tent, and the silver under it."*

Covetousness produces only negative results like theft, lying, murder, harmful lusts, and apostasy. Only sorrow comes from covetousness—and eventually death, if it is allowed to dominate a person's mind.

It is reminiscent of (**2 Thessalonians 2**) and the man of sin. Apostasy is taking place, and God says that He was going to allow delusion to come upon people, a "blindness" to occur. A similar thing happened to Solomon. When we add what is taught in 2 Thessalonians, we find that the blindness is, in reality, self-imposed.

God did not make Solomon blind, and He will not make the people spoken of in 2 Thessalonians 2 blind either. But, because of their behavior, neither will He stop their progression towards it. It is not that the people utterly refuse to accept truth—just as Solomon never renounced God. The problem is that they do not love it!

The problem is one of dedication. What was Solomon dedicated to? He was not dedicated to God for very long after his good beginning. He was dedicated to his projects—to building Jerusalem, the Temple, his home, botanical gardens—things that only expanded his overwhelming vanity.

He ignored the laws God gave for kings (**Deuteronomy 17:14-20**), and that was sin. Unfortunately, unlike David, Solomon did not have the spiritual resources to recover from what he did. David recovered when he sinned because he had a relationship with God. Even though he sinned, he would bounce back from it in repentance.

(**1 Kings 11:4**) says that Solomon "*clung to*" his wives. Normally, that would be good. A man should cling or cleave to his wife. Solomon, though, cleaved to the wrong women, and his attachment to them led him astray. As he tolerated their worship of other gods right in his home, his resistance wore down, and he became increasingly vulnerable. Before long, he was participating in the worship of their gods. Once he was accustomed to it, it wore away his loyalty as each compromise made the next step easier. His vanity deceived him into feeling that his strength and resolve were so great that he would not fall. But he did, and he paid a bitter price.

One of the deceptive aspects to what Solomon did is something that any of us could fall prey to. It does not have to be foreign women or something like an all-consuming hobby. Religion, however, especially entrapped him through his wives.

Virtually every religion uses similar terminology. Every Christian sect uses the terms "born again," "salvation," "saved," and "redemption." We could add "justification," "mercy," "kindness," "forgiveness," and "grace." All Western religions (and maybe now even some of these New Age religions) share some of the same terminology, but the theology behind the terms is radically different.

In Solomon's day, the religions of Ashtoreth, Molech, Baal, Chemosh, and the other false gods used terminology very similar to what was being used in Israel, but the theology was vastly different. This is what trapped Solomon. Once a comfortable syncretism is accepted, God is gradually neglected and idolatry is adopted. Thomas Jefferson is credited with saying, "The price of liberty is eternal vigilance." This is just as true in regard to religion as it is to civil liberty under a government.

Apostasy

(**1Kings 12:25-33**) records the beginning of the Kingdom of Israel's apostasy. Fearing that he might eventually lose political control over the ten tribes because of their long-standing religious ties to Jerusalem, capital of the Kingdom of Judah (verse 27), Jeroboam 1st instituted a state religion designed to meet his peoples' needs for convenience - and his own need for power. He built two shrines, one in Bethel, at the southern extremity of his kingdom, the other in Dan, near its northern boundary (verse 29). If not de jure, at least de facto, he exiled the Levites, the priestly tribe established by God, and installed in their place a priesthood of his own devising (verse 31). Finally, he moved the fall holy day season from the seventh month to the eighth, thereby effectively setting aside the Sabbath commandment, since the holy days are God's Sabbaths see (**Leviticus 23:1-3, 23-44**). All this "*became a sin*" for Israel (**1 Kings 12:30**).

Jeroboam's apostasy, his movement to false religious practices, took deep root. In fact, the house of Israel never departed from the practices he established.

(**2 Kings 17:21-23**) records this fact: *"For he rent Israel from the house of David; and they made Jeroboam the son of Nebat king: and Jeroboam drave Israel from following the LORD, and made them sin a great sin. For the children of Israel walked in all the sins of Jeroboam which he did; they departed not from them; Until the LORD removed Israel out of his sight, as he had said by all his servants the prophets. So was Israel carried away out of their own land to Assyria unto this day."*

Jeroboam drove Israel from following the LORD, and made them commit a great sin. For the children of Israel walked in all the sins of Jeroboam which he did; they did not depart from them, until the LORD removed Israel out of His sight.

Having abandoned the Sabbath, the God-given sign marking them as His people (**Exodus 31:13-17**), the folk of the northern tribes eventually lost their identification. That is why most Israelites do not know who they are to this day. The forefathers forsook the sign that denoted their connection to God.

Take this line of thought to its logical conclusion: The Sabbath is a memorial to creation and, by extension, to the Creator God see (**Exodus 20:11**). Modern-day Israelites do not know who they are today because their forefathers, generations ago, abandoned this memorial to the Creator God. Therefore, modern-day Israelites have come to abandon more than the sign: They have abandoned the God to whom the sign points. They no longer know God.

This is not an overstatement. Make no mistake: Failure to recognize who Israel is today is failure to recognize the God who made Israel! The distressing secularism running rampant in the modern nations of Israel today has its roots in Sabbath-breaking. The antidote for secularism in America is not an inane Constitutional amendment requiring the teaching of creationism in the state schools. The panacea some offer, prayer in the public schools, will not do the trick. Increased Sunday church attendance will not stanch the flood of secularism; after all, most Sunday worshippers accept the doctrines of biologic and economic determinism (i.e., evolution and socialism, respectively) just as avowed atheists do. Attempting to unite a people with its God through these measures is surely akin to building a wall with "untendered mortar" see (**Ezekiel 13:9-23**). In the coming storm, such a wall will fall.

However, one will never find a Sabbath-keeper who is a secularist, for the Sabbath-keeper has maintained his link with the Creator God. Sabbath-keeping and secularism mix about as well as oil and water.

Paul writes in Ephesians that a Christian can stand firm in god's way if he is properly equipped.

(**Ephesians 6:16**) *"Above all, taking the shield of faith, wherewith ye shall be able to quench all the fiery darts of the wicked."* Satan throws multiple distractions, trials, and ideas at God's children, and without the strength of faith, these can quickly and easily engulf us and make our heads spin. Without protection, their intensity could take our eternal life!

The Bible frequently speaks of spiritual lethargy and apostasy in terms of disease. He says of Judah.

(**Isaiah 1:5-6**) *"Why should ye be stricken anymore? Ye will revolt more and more: the whole head is sick, and the whole heart faint. From the sole of the foot even unto the head, there is no soundness in it; but wounds, and bruises, and putrefying sores: they have not been closed, neither bound up, neither mollified with ointment."*

In fact David writes in the Psalm.

(**Psalm 38:3**) *"There is no soundness in my flesh because of thine anger; neither is there any rest in my bones because of my sin."*

Jesus uses this metaphor as well:

(**Mark 2:17**) *"When Jesus heard it, he saith unto them, They that are whole have no need of a physician, but they that are sick: I come not to call the righteous, but sinners, to repentance."*

Most telling is Christ's instruction to the spiritually blind Laodicean church.

(**Revelation 3:18**) *"anoint thine eyes with eye salve that you may see."*

Applying this biblical metaphor to the events of (**2 Kings 4**), the boy, representing the individual Christian, falls prey to prolonged exposure to Satan's world. Since the tender, inexperienced child is unprepared for the onslaught of such a powerful and intense foe, the Devil easily overcomes his resistance, and his mother can only watch her child die in her arms. How many of our former brethren have we helplessly watched "die" in the arms of the church in recent years?

Yes, the body of Christ, the church, has been sick—from top to bottom. It was not just the leadership that went astray. It is all of us.

By refusing to repent of their apostasy from God's way of life, the Israelites could only expect the coming of God's fearsome punishment. The people of Israel would recognize these words as a funeral dirge, a lamentation said over the dead. Amos speaks, not as if it were yet to occur, but as if it had already happened. This death came when Assyria conquered

Israel from 721 to 718 BC and deported her people to foreign lands.

Why?

Anciently, only the Jews, along with their Israelite brethren, were the recipients of God's revelation:

(**Amos 3:2**) "*You only have I known of all the families of the earth: therefore I will punish you for all your iniquities'.*"

God counts that revelation as a precious blessing to the family of Abraham, as Paul writes in Romans.

(**Romans 3:1-2**) "*What advantage then hath the Jew? Or what is the profit of circumcision? Much in every way! Chiefly because to them were committed the oracles of God.*"

To Paul, the Jews were not cursed, but were first, the Greeks second (**Romans 2:9-10**). He took seriously his commission to carry God's name.

(**Acts 9:15**) "*But the Lord said unto him. Go thy way: for he is a chosen vessel unto me, to bear my name before the Gentiles, and Kings, and the children of Israel.*"

The book of Acts records that in every town and city he visited, he went first to the local Jewish synagogue; after that, he preached the gospel to the Gentiles. Indeed, he admonished the church at Thessalonica to.

(**1 Thessalonians 2:14**) "*For ye, brethren, become followers of the churches of God which in Judaea are in Christ Jesus: for ye also have suffered like things of your own countrymen, even as they have of the Jews:*"

God gave the Jews a lot. Here, the principle enters the picture:

(**Luke 12:48**) "*But he that knew not, and did commit things worthy of stripes, shall be beaten with few stripes. For unto whomsoever much is given, of him shall be much required: and to whom men have committed much, of him they will ask the more.*"

As we know from the Old Testament and as history since have demonstrated, the Jews have repeatedly rejected God, treading His oracles underfoot. Today, many are the Jews who have forsaken God and joined the vanguard of liberal secularism in the arts, law, politics, science, education— in virtually every field of human endeavor. Throughout their history, many Jews have scorned God's revelation, purposefully making themselves a profane people. So, the corollary of Christ's principle applies, as stated in

Luke.

(**Luke 12:47**) *"And that servant, which knew his lord's will, and not prepared not himself, neither did according to his will, shall be beaten with many stripes."*

The Jews, more than any single people in history, knew God's will, as it is expressed in the "oracles"—His revelation to them. They often have rejected it. As often as they do, their apostasy has carried with it the penalty of "many stripes."

(**Acts 20:28-31**) *"Take heed therefore unto yourselves, and to all the flock, over the which the Holy Ghost hath made you overseers, to feed the church of God, which he hath purchased with his own blood. For I know this, that after my departing shall grievous wolves enter in among you, not sparing the flock. Also of your own selves shall men arise, speaking perverse things, to draw away disciples after them. Therefore watch, and remember, that by the space of three years I ceased not to warn every one night and day with tears."*

Paul's address here to the Ephesians elders probably took place in the springtime of AD 56. His prophecies to them of apostasy and corrupt leadership that Peter, Jude, and John would later write about as it was happening.

(**Acts 20:29**) *"For I know this that after my departing shall grievous wolves enter in among you, not sparing the flock."*

He calls these future apostates, these future false teachers, "savage wolves." Jude later calls them "brute beasts."

(**Jude 1:10**) *"But these speak evil of those things which they know not: but what they know naturally, as brute beasts, in those things they corrupt themselves."*

This conjures in our minds the idea that man's animalistic nature—what one could call the physical side of man's nature, what he shares with the beasts—is driving these false teachers. It is not necessarily their minds and their ideas that are driving them but their bodies, their desires, their lusts, and they want these lusts satiated in some way. It is not just eating, drinking, sex, and similar carnal needs, but also the base desires that men have for gain, for standing atop the pack, for glory and prestige. These false teachers are letting their "animal nature" get the best of them.

(**Acts 20:29-30**) *"For I know this, that after my departing shall grievous wolves enter* *in among you, not sparing the flock. Also of your own selves shall men arise, speaking perverse things, to draw away disciples after them."*

Paul specifically says these apostates will rise up from among the ministry. In verse 29, he says that "*savage wolves will come in among you,*" and in verse 30, that "*among yourselves men will rise up.*" They will be people in leadership positions or those who are considered to be pillars in the church and highly respected. Thus, they are in an advantageous position, from their point of view, to do the most damage.

Judgments and criticisms from the world

(**1 Corinthians 2:9-16**) "*But as it is written, Eye hath not seen, nor ear heard, neither have entered into the heart of man, the things which God hath prepared for them that love him. But God hath revealed them unto us by his Spirit: for the Spirit seracheth all things, yea, the deep things of God. For what man knoweth the things of a man, save the spirit of man which is in him? Even so the things of God knoweth no man, but the Spirit of God. Now we have received, not the spirit of the world, but the spirit which is of God; that we might know the things that are freely given to us of God. Which things also we speak, not in the words which man's wisdom teacheth, but which the Holy Ghost teacheth; comparing spiritual things with spiritual. But the natural man receiveth not the things of the Spirit of God: for they are foolishness unto him: neither can he know them, because they are spiritually discerned. But he that is spiritual judgeth all things, yet he himself is judged of no man. For who hath known the mind of the Lord, that he may instruct him? But we have the mind of Christ.*"

The verb Paul uses in verse 10, translated "revealed" (Greek apokalupto), is a strong term, usually used in the New Testament to indicate divine revelation of certain supernatural secrets or with the resurrection and judgment of certain people and events. These verses in (**1 Corinthians 2**) stress the work of the Holy Spirit in revealing the wisdom of God.

In verse 14, the verb *anakrino*, translated "discerned," is the same verb translated "judges" and "judged" in verse 15. The idea in each case is to make intelligent, spiritual decisions. *Anakrino*, though meaning "examine," includes the decision following the examination.

Members of God's church are to examine all things, including our own lives, with the help of God's Spirit, and then we are to make an evaluation as to what our strengths and weaknesses are. Then we decide what we are going to do about them. No one in the world has a right to examine and evaluate us on spiritual matters because, without the Holy Spirit, they cannot rightly and justly understand or evaluate. There is no need to feel slighted or put down by anyone in the world who disagrees with God's truth or with your obedience to God's truth. The same holds true in all judgments and criticisms from the world - that is, those without God's Holy Spirit - who try to tell us our doctrines are wrong.

This is a major reason the Worldwide Church of God went into apostasy, because the leaders believed and accepted the criticisms of the worldly churches. They accepted judgment from people without God's Holy Spirit and from organizations without a spiritual foundation of truth.

Today's mainstream Christian churches are worldly, they are not led by people with the Holy Spirit, and they do not base their doctrines on truth. Do not be fooled by mainstream Christianity's false piety! They are not God's people. They are not baptized members of God's church. They do not have God's Holy Spirit. This is not to say that there are not wonderful people in some of these churches in the world. In addition, when they do follow some of God's laws, blessings will automatically accrue to them.

The Law's Purpose and Intent

(**2 Corinthians 11:1-4**) "*Would to God ye could bear with me a little in my folly: and indeed bear with me. For I am jealous over you with godly jealousy: for I have espoused you to one husband that I may present you as a chaste virgin to Christ. But I fear, lest by any means, as the serpent beguiled Eve through his subtlety, so your minds should be corrupted from the simplicity that is in Christ. For if he that cometh preacheth another Jesus, whom we have not preached, or if ye receive another spirit, which ye have not received, or another gospel, which ye have not accepted, ye might well bear with him.*"

Paul had to deal with the Corinthian congregation because they had fallen under the sway of false apostles.

(**2 Corinthians 11:13**) "*For such are false apostles, deceitful workers, transforming themselves into the apostles of Christ.*"

These false ministers had convinced many of the brethren that they knew more and better than the apostle through whom they had heard, believed, learned, and been converted to the gospel. They were in the process of throwing aside what they had learned from Paul in favor of what they were hearing from these new "apostles."

Damnable Heresies

(**Galatians 3:4**) "*Have ye suffered so many things in vain? If it be yet in vain.*"

There were a number of accepted belief systems in Palestine and the greater Roman Empire at the time this was written, such as Gnosticism and Judaism, but it is certain that God's truth was never popular or widely accepted. It is practically a foregone conclusion that someone practicing the truth will be persecuted for it to one degree or another. C.f. (**Matthew 13:21; Romans 8:35-36; Galatians 5:11; 2 Timothy 3:12; 1 Peter 2:19-21**)

In fact, the churches of Galatia may have been forewarned about this by Paul when he was teaching in Derbe, Lystra, Iconium, and Antioch (all on the south-eastern border of Galatia) as recorded in (**Acts 14:20-22**). Christians are called to be separate from this world and its ways, and when the world recognizes this difference, it lashes out.

From Paul's writing, it seems that the Galatians had the proper foundation at one time, and they really did understand the truth at the beginning of their spiritual lives. This would have been the time when they were actively standing up for the truth, and a great contrast would have been evident between the Galatians and the general population. This is when they would have suffered - in the internal struggle of having to give up their former conduct, or with the external struggle of not fitting in with the rest of society.

As the Galatians began to slide into apostasy, they would no longer have been so repulsive to the people around them, and the suffering and persecution would have begun to lessen - the world would have started to recognize itself in them again.

(**John 15:19**) *"If ye were of the world, the world would love his own: but because ye are not of the world, but I have chosen you out of the world, therefore the world hateth you."*

In essence, Paul is asking them if they are just going to throw away all that they had learned especially what they had learned through adversity. With this question he is pointing out that, if they fall away, everything they had been through, both good and bad, would have been in vain in the sense that there would be no future profit from it. They would have received the maximum benefit from it already. This relates to:

(**Romans 8:28**) *"And we know that all things work together for good to them that love God, to them who are the called according to his purpose."*

Where we are promised that all that we suffer will be redeemed for those who meet the requirements listed - those who are called according to His purpose, which the Galatians ostensibly were, and those who love God, which the Galatians were not doing in that they were relegating Christ's sacrifice for sin as meaningless.

(**Philippians 1:27**) *"Only let your conversation be as it becometh the gospel of Christ: that whether I come and see you, or else be absent, I may hear of your affairs, that ye stand fast in one spirit, with one mind striving together for the faith of the gospel;"*

Paul wrote this to the Philippian church, considered to be one of his better, most beloved congregations, before the major apostasy of the late first century hit full stride. However, he was already beginning to warn them that they needed to be united in one spirit and one mind and strive, show some effort, work hard, to keep the unity of the faith.

(**2 Thessalonians 2:1-2**) *"Now we beseech you, brethren, by the coming of our Lord Jesus Christ, and by our gathering together unto him, That ye be not soon shaken in mind, or be troubled, neither by spirit, nor by word, nor by letter as from us, as that the day of Christ is at hand."*

Already some had lost heart to the point that they were saying, "Christ has already come. He is here on earth." So they had little to look forward to.

(**2 Thessalonians 2:3**) *"Let no man deceive you by any means: for that day shall not come, except there come a falling away first, and that man of sin be revealed, the son of perdition;"*

Apostasy ("the falling away") is not necessarily a departure from an organized body but a departure from truth, as the context shows. It points to a deliberate abandonment of a former professed position or belief.

The Flood Is Upon Us!

Some think that, when someone accepts heresy, he will "leave the church." That may occur on some occasions, but this confuses hairesis with apostasia. In this verse, apostasia is translated "falling away" in both the KJV and NKJV, giving the impression that it refers to leaving an organization. But apostasia means "to depart from truth"! One can remain in an organization and be departing from truth all along.

This is vitally important to us living at the end time! Notice what Paul writes about this:

(**2 Thessalonians 2:9-12**) *"Even him, whose coming is after the working of Satan with all power and signs and lying wonders, And with all deceivableness of unrighteousness in them that perish; because they received not the love of the truth, that they might be saved. And for this cause God shall send them strong delusion, that they should believe a lie: That they all might be damned who believed not the truth, but had pleasure in unrighteousness."*

10 THEN WHEN AND HOW OF APOSTASY

The Removing of the Lamp stand

John writes in Revelation about the removing of the lamp stand:

(**Revelation 1:12-13**) "*And I turned to see the voice that spake with me. And being turned, I saw seven golden candlesticks; and in the midst of the seven candlesticks one like unto the Son of man, clothed with a garment down to the foot, and girt about the paps with a golden girdle.*"

Here John sees Christ glorified in his holy priestly garb. He is seen walking among the seven branches Menorah, like the Menorah in the Holy Place in the tabernacle. The fuel for its light was pure olive oil, which it needed to burn properly. This oil was to be fed into the lamp stand and burn continuously on behalf of the children of Israel.

The lamp stand in the Old Testament symbolized Jesus as the Light of the World that was to burn continually, giving its light in the Holy Place where the priest would be see (**John 1:7-9, 8:12, 9:5, 12:46; 2 Corinthians 4:6; Luke 1:78-79, 2:32; Revelation 21:23-24**). The responsibility of the priests was to keep the lamp burning. They had to feed it oil and trim its wicks so it would not smoke, but continue to burn without failing to give pure light.

It also symbolized the believer, in that the believer is also called the light of the World (**Matthew 5:14-17**). After Jesus ascended into heaven c.f. (**John 9:5; Philippians 2:15; Luke 12:35; Ephesians 5:8-9**) the believer is also called the light of the world (**Matthew 5:14-17**). For that reason the believer is also to walk in the light, i.e., His Word (**1 John 1:7**). Therefore the lamp stand can also be seen as a symbol of the Church, bringing the light to a world of darkness as representatives of Christ.

We see this motif continuing:

(**Revelation 1:20**) *"The mystery of the seven stars which thou sawest in my right hand, and the seven golden candlesticks. The seven stars are the angels of the seven churches, and the seven candlesticks which thou sawest are the seven churches."*

This tells us the seven stars are the angels of the seven churches. Whenever the word stars is used symbolically, it refers to angels. The seven candlesticks are seven churches of which Christ is the head. Just as the oil lit the Menorah (lamp stand), so does the Holy Spirit illumine all the Churches. The seven individual candlesticks symbolize the seven local churches which represent the whole of the Church, not just different ages of the Church. (**Revelation 1:4**) said they already existed in Asia at the time of the writing of Revelation; they were not just future churches or representative of Church ages only. We can concede that these churches are examples of churches throughout all ages and that all seven can exist at the same time in type, as they have throughout history. The last church mentioned is Laodicea, during the latter times the Laodicean church would be dominant one. It is this Church that will be common in the end time and will usher in the apostasy.

(**Revelation 2:1**) *"Unto the angel of the church of Ephesus write, these things saith He who holdeth the seven stars in His right hand, who walketh in the midst of the seven golden candlesticks;"*

The Lord walks among the churches in all ages to know them. Jesus commends and rebukes them and gives a specific warning to this church.

(**Revelation 2:5**) *"Remember therefore from whence thou art fallen, repent, and do the first works; or else I will come to thee quickly, and will remove thou candlestick out of his place, except thou repent."*

The removing of the church candlestick meant Christ's Spirit would depart and leave them on their own, which in turn would result in them being as Laodicea (Laodicea means men's opinions ruling in place of God). Loyalty to Christ can and often is replaced by loyalty to an organization, a church, and its leaders, substituting new rules and interpretations for Biblical truths. We can see this example in cults.

We find that all the churches mentioned in Revelation exist at the same time, and we can find the faithful Church existing alongside the unfaithful Church today. But there is only one Church that will take over that will become the center of apostasy. The church of Laodicea has prepared the way for the great apostasy. It has kept Christ out of the Church and from

His people. It has stood for nothing for so long that it has little effect on society, while at the same time it has allowed anything contrary to Christ's teachings to come in. Today the world looks at this Church and excuses its sin, because there is no salt left for conviction. This Church became lukewarm, seeking unity with everyone, showing tolerance for any doctrinal aberration and interpreting it as love. It is reflective of a Church that at end of the age has come under the influence of the world instead of being an influence in the world. No wonder the world wonders why it should be judged if there is no substantial difference between it and the Church. But judgment begins in the House of God. The Lord is infinitely more concerned about His people than about the unbeliever. And so Jesus commends, warns and rebukes each church. Because God removes His candlestick from apostate churches they have resorted to worldly methods and techniques in order to continue to attract people. After all, one must keep the organizational wheels rolling!

The Laodicean church thought they were doing well and were spiritual. After all they were rich, so of course God must be blessing them. The wealthy mostly dress well and talk about their possessions to impress people. They focus on outward appearances and worldliness. But these people did not know their inward condition; they were blind and could not see. So the Lord asked if they would buy from Him gold refined in the fire (by their suffering) white garments (robes of salvation) and eye salve so they could see their condition. Today many see their success and prosperity as God's blessing. The Laodicean Church was lukewarm. The Lord wanted them either cold or hot. Hot water was used for healing; cold was used for refreshment. Instead, they could not make up their mind; they were standing for nothing, and were good for nothing. They lived in both worlds. Spiritually they could have been either all for God or not at all, but they were in between. If they were hot, they would have been approved. If they were cold, God could have changed them, but they were in the middle and He was unable do anything. This is the worst place to be, to be part of a church, doing church things, thinking you are a Christian when in fact you are not. The Laodicean had just enough religiosity to get by and think they were fine. They were naked also. In the time of Christ all soldiers would sleep in their clothes, they would not take them off so they would be ready for battle. We are to be clothed in white garments, the righteousness of Christ. Jesus was saying they did not have his righteousness they were naked. Yet even this church is not hopeless; Christ can come in to the individual if He is allowed, as many as I love, I rebuke and chasten. Therefore be zealous and repent. This is the only Church that He is outside of and offers to come to the individual in the Church and not the collective Church. Because the whole Church is removed from the truth, and is not functioning in the word of God. This does not mean they abandon Gods word or name but only use portions of it that suit them, or change its meaning.

Many have identified the Apostasy as individuals departing from God.

Certainly over the centuries many individuals that had begun in the Church left and started their own cult. However, this is only part of the picture as Jesus is addressing the Church He personally walks among them. In modern times this falling away had started in liberal seminaries that sent teachers out to unsuspecting pulpits teaching their liberal ideas-- those who promote homosexuality, who ordain people that deny the Trinity, the deity of Christ, the virgin birth and the essentials of the faith. Then the new age movement began to emerge and infiltrate the Church with kingdom dominion theology and placing subjective experience over the authority of the objective Word of God. Then the homosexual movement came through the Episcopal Church along with feminists who disdain God as father. Now this apostasy has become something so widespread it encompasses most things that are considered sacred. Affecting almost all denominations to some degree that doctrines are distorted and abandoned, controlling shepherds are in charge, teaching coveting, wealth and perfect health as Gods will to all. They approve of divorce and accept homosexuality.

A little leaven leavened the whole

Among the parables of the kingdom (**Matthew 13**) is the parable of the leaven,

(**Matthew 13:33**) *"Another parable spake he unto them; The kingdom of heaven is like unto leaven, which a woman took, and hid in three measures of meal, till the whole was leavened."*

This depicts the course of this present Church age. It describes a progression of apostasy that radically escalates in the end. Apostasy refers to falling away from the true Faith which finds its instruction by God's word. Jesus describes a woman putting leaven into three measures of meal, until the whole was leavened. Leaven puffs up; it represents pride, it does the opposite of what the gospel does which humbles man and makes us God-reliant. Paul said A little leaven leavens the whole lump. Leaven in Scripture stands for sin and false teaching see (**1 Corinthians 5:6; Galatians 5:9**), and the woman represents the Church. She did something God prohibits; she hid the leaven in the meal, mingling a foreign element into the body. This is speaking of a corrupting influence that would infiltrate all parts of the Church. As a little yeast, is hidden in the flour. It works silently until all the mass is brought under its influence. It shows evil existing till the end of the age, as things do not get better but worse. The parable tells us that the error which was first introduced by false teachers during the days of the Apostles (and was then small), will gradually increase through the centuries until, at the end, it is completed. And almost the entire Church will have been impacted in some way. By this characterization of leaven in the meal, believers are warned that false teaching will gradually increase through time until the entire church has been affected in some way. The ultimate fulfillment of this falling away is found in Revelation 17.

The Timing of the Apostasy

Paul writes to the Thessalonians about those who have tried to deceive them with a false teaching on the Tribulation that was upsetting the church. Apparently after Paul left Thessalonica some false teachers came in and upset the church by teaching that believers were now in the Tribulation.

(**2 Thessalonians 2:1-2**) *"Now we beseech you, brethren, by the coming of our Lord Jesus Christ, and by our gathering together unto him, That ye be not soon shaken in mind, or be troubled, neither by spirit, nor by word, nor by letter as from us, as that the day of Christ is at hand."*

They were being told that the Day of the Lord had come and that the rapture and resurrection had occurred, putting them in the Tribulation The Day of the Lord is the most common title for the Great Tribulation see (**1 Timothy 1:20; 2 Timothy 2:18**).

The main point of Paul's letter was to comfort the believers of Thessalonica who were already experiencing persecution (first letter) and also correct those, letting them know that they were not in the Tribulation. Paul then wanted to clarify what would precede the Tribulation. He pointed out that the mystery of lawlessness was still being restrained, and because of this the Antichrists unveiling was still in the future, prior to Christ's return. The Antichrist would be revealed at that time.

Paul's correction to the Church at Thessalonica came with the warning Let no one deceive you. It should seem obvious that Paul was not writing about our gathering together to Him - Christ (v.3) before that day. This gathering will not come first without two things happening prior to that:

        1. The falling away would come first (then the day comes).

2. The man of sin would be revealed.

Here Paul is obviously talking about two different matters: our gathering together to Him and a falling away. Paul states that the Day of the Lord will not come without the Apostasy coming first; that prior to Christ's coming a falling away from the Faith will occur. Therefore he warns us who are living at the time, Let no one deceive you, giving the same warning Jesus did in the beginning of his discourse in (**Matthew 24**).

As Paul mentions the coming of our Lord Jesus and also our gathering together to Him, he appears to be indicating two events, distinguishing between two comings of Jesus (**1 Thessalonians 3:13**), tells us that when Jesus comes it is with the saints who have died. One coming is for His Church and the other with His Church, when He will judge a rebellious world and set up His kingdom reign on earth for 1,000 years with the saints under Him co-reigning.

(**2 Thessalonians 2:1**) *"Now we beseech you, brethren, by the coming of our Lord Jesus Christ, and by our gathering together unto him."*

Our gathering together to Him. The Greek word for gathering together is epi synagogues. Epi means above, and synagogues means to collect together, this is not a reference to our being gathered to Jesus after He descends to earth to set up His kingdom, but to our being gathered up to Him. We are called FROM ABOVE by the Lord to meet Him and be united together in the air and brought to the place He has already prepared see (**John 14**). Our gathering together up to Him is more accurately translated as our being gathered UP to Him see (**1 Thessalonians 4:14**). He is the object we go to; He does not come down to meet us on earth, we go up to Him first.

It hasn't been until modern times that the Rapture has been abandoned for earthly triumphalism and Christianizing the World first, before Christ could come. (Kingdom Now, Dominion Theology) This is all part of the falling away and not preparing or watching for His coming.

(**2 Thessalonians 2:3**) *"Let no man deceive you by any means: for that Day shall not come, except there come a falling away first, and that man of sin be revealed, the son of perdition;"*

In (**Matthew 24:4**) Christ first warned of the deception of those who come in His name three times, but He also speaks of what will occur before the Abomination of Desolation.

By definition Paul is giving a warning, just like Christ did. Paul refers to tricks of any kind, saying to be on guard. Christ's return will not occur before certain important things take place, so the timing is important. In (**2 Thessalonians 2:3**) in the phrase the falling away the word *Apostasia* is used, which comes from the Greek verb *aphistemi*, which literally means, to depart or revolt. Paul spoke of another departure (**1Timothy 4:1**) and used the same Greek word. However, in 1 Timothy Paul added the words depart from the faith instead of depart by itself, qualifying the phrase. Paul states the reason for their falling away: because they are listening to demons, who are deceiving spirits. So they are being deceived by teachings that are contrary to the word of God and this is occurring inside the Church.

Concerning the coming of Our Lord Jesus Christ and our gathering together unto Him, will not happen until AFTER the Apostasy occurs. There is no other way to understand these words without changing the context for the words and the grammatical construction of this verse. Those who teach prophecy will rarely touch on this all-encompassing event, the falling away from the faith. Why not, when this falling away or apostasy is the main indication of the Church's condition in the last hour? It will affect the Church more than anything else in history, but it is ignored and even questioned as a possible event. How can you teach on end time prophecy without it?

The apostasy of professing Christianity has increased with a momentum that is stunning to those watching its growth. It has gone off the Richter scale. In the absence of the candlesticks (the presence of Christ), the devil has stepped in and taken over in many churches. This falling away has certainly begun and is picking up momentum each year, month, and week. Whole movements have arisen that draw huge crowds by catering to the natural mans desires and prey on his propensity of being deceived by the supernatural. They are being offered the very things Christ refused and warned against in his teachings.

The conflict that the Church once had with the World has been embraced and brought into the church. It has created a sharp division between traditional biblical purists and new revelation revivalists and liberal Christianity.

How did this all Happen?

I have already touched in general on the Church in the 21th Century and the development of divergent tributaries all flowing away from the word of God. But for us as individuals, apostasy specifically begins with indifference, holding no convictions, and having no boldness for the truth; and so we become men pleasers and lovers of the World, instead of lovers of God and His truth. In time it becomes nothing short than a total abandonment of Christ and His teachings.

The Scripture tells us in the end times the love of many will grow cold.

In (**Matthew 24**) Jesus' explains this is because of lawlessness and not heeding His word.

Loving people enough to confront them when the truth is abandoned and the doctrines are changed to fit the culture. The Laodicean church had slowly been losing its first love and the result was not obeying the Lord's commands: occupy until I come and teach them the truth (discipleship). Open mindedness and the acceptance of any doctrine for the sake of unity is worldly tolerance, and not a display of real love. But Laodicea boasts in its riches and how well off they are. The best of times for the Church is the cry, sound familiar.

While history has shown the growth of various apostasies by cults springing up by those who left the Church. (There is evidence of both in the End Times: Read (**1Timothy 4:1-3 and 2 Timothy 3:1-5; 4:3-4**), the Scriptures point to an apostasy among those who once followed God who are still in the church. It is a world-wide rebellion, not just a few but many. The article in the verse makes it even more significant; this is not a falling away, but the falling away, the great and final rebellion against God, his word and ruler ship in individual lives, and churches. It's a departure from His word and a replacement by another's. This is different from error, which results from ignorance. Although it does includes false beliefs and error. The motivation is willful and it defies what the Word states because of an adherence to its own deception.

How does a group of Christians or a whole church that loves the Lord fall away? By not adhering to the commands found in the Word. The Scriptures are put aside for agendas and other activities. Paul warns of false teachers rising up from among the church, and being on our guard against worldliness. All too often today's Church measures success by size and popularity, just as the Bible said it would in the end. It begins with just a small compromise and from there it is just a matter of time before one doesn't even realize they can't even find the place they have drifted from. Without an anchor the tide takes us where it wants.

(**1 Timothy 4:1**) *"Now the Spirit speaketh expressly, that in latter times some will depart from the faith, giving heed to deceiving spirits and doctrines of devils;"*

Notice that some will depart from the faith, not all. Tolerance has been the main cause of leaving any absolutes in the Word of God. We simply do not love the truth more than other things and it eventually comes to be replaced with what can only be identified as lies. Lies can be disguised and embraced because they are easier to comprehend than the truth which takes good soil to be sowed in.

God has commanded that His people separate from error not to join in with it. People who reject this command eventually find themselves on the side of apostasy. How can it be possible then, that God is now calling for the walls of separation to be broken down? This is not the great commission but the great confusion which will continually grow into the great apostasy.

James says where there is confusion every evil thing is there. Today's ecumenical tolerance in the name of love and unity has made much of the Church depart from the truth which subsequently has left it with little power. It has not brought what so many have promised. For example those who wanted to unite in mission with the Roman Catholic Church for social change now find themselves in a predicament, as the Pope has recently been photographed kissing the Koran (inside the Vatican). If we continue to wink at falsehood we will eventually shut our eyes to the truth. See (**Romans 16:17, 18; 2 Corinthians 6:14-18; 1 Timothy 1:3; 2 Timothy 2:16-21, 3:5, 13; Titus 1:10-13; 3:9-11; 2 John 7-11; Revelation 18:4**)

Eventually a last day's apostate Church, along with the rest of the world will accept the Mark of the Beast as an allegiance to global unity; it may even become a deterrent to terrorism. This mark comes to be a required in the middle of the Tribulation, so there is no way to identify it with now. However it is obvious that a system will need to be implemented to further economic unity and global monetary success. Revelation 13 tells us that no one will be able to buy or sell without the mark. Today it is very hard to do any business without computers throughout most of the world.

Numerous mass population identification and tracking systems have been developed, such as an implantable chip or a transponder placed in a plastic wristband. This Identification and Tracking technology will be used in the New World order system for the global economy. Right now on the books the US has a patent for a number tattoo for everyone in America. There is also a patent for a digital transceiver chip called digital angel. This is a implantable transceiver that sends and receives data and can be continuously tracked by GPS (Global Positioning Satellite) When implanted within a body, the device is powered electromechanically through the movement of muscles, and it can be activated either by the wearer or by the monitoring facility. A novel sensation feedback feature will even allow the wearer to control the device to some degree. The smart device is also small enough to be hidden inconspicuously on or within valuable personal belongings (On December 10, 1999, Applied Digital Solutions, Inc. (ADS) acquired the patent rights to this technology, which the company refers to as Digital Angel On May 10, 2002 it became the official day to be implanted in humans. Several have already volunteered and taken the chip. The technology is here, it only waits for a certain individual who will bring it all together.

Then there is the Signs and Wonders Movement, from the promise of miracle debt cancellation to confessing to posses it by the words you speak.

This movement is motivated by coveting, promising power so that you can change reality by manipulation in the spiritual realm. Supernatural experiences are plainly one of the glues which hold together the end-time apostasy. Paul addressed the Ephesians elders:

(**Acts 20:29-30**) *"For I know this that after my departing shall grievous wolves enter in among you, not sparing the flock. Also of your own selves shall men arise, speaking perverse things, to draw away disciples after them."*

Many flock to see their favorite teacher and see his miracle working power televised. Jesus said that deceiving signs and wonders will be an integral part of the last-days deception to the Church.

This is not the time to hide ones head in the sand, hoping that it will all go away; it won't. If we really believe the apostasy comes first and that the time we are living in is the Laodicean church age, then we are that much closer to the Lord's coming. It can literally be the last moments of time before a tribulation period, the most disastrous time the earth has ever seen. We should be hard at work, before the night falls. As the saying goes, you don't play in the last quarter of a football game like you do in the first quarter. And this is no game! It is for the eternal destiny of souls, your friends and loved ones. Time to awake to your calling in Christ.

(**2 Thessalonians 2:7**) *"For the mystery of iniquity* (lawlessness) *doth already work: only He who now letteth will let, until He be taken out of the way."*

Once the restraining power is removed the Scripture says another HE will be revealed. The he is the Antichrist the Son of Perdition who will flood the World with his false teaching and signs and wonders to conquer them. Paul used James and Jambres as an example of miracle opposition for what will occur in the last days.

How is this possible? One of the ways is through TV. The Lord never said the gospel would be preached in all the World through the medium of TV, but through people. Those who were willing to give up their lives and go on the mission field of the World. It should be obvious to anyone who watches Christian TV that most do not give up anything as in the first century but actually gain the World's pleasures by going. The lines are being drawn today with those who follow the crowd as sheep and those who follow the Master as His sheep. However there is hope as there has always been a remnant.

This apostasy cannot be just the continuance of the same things that were always wrong. Paul uses it as a signpost for the coming of the Lord for his Church and the nearness of the tribulation! In order to be a sign, it has to be DIFFERENT from anything else that has occurred. But it will not notice by all because the majority will be part of it.

(**2 Thessalonians 2:9**) *"Even him, whose coming is after the working of Satan with all power and signs and lying wonders,"*

The coming of the lawless one is according to the working of Satan, with all power, signs, and lying wonders i.e., the energy and power of Satan with full and complete strength to have the ability to work signs and wonders.

(**Matthew 24:24**) *"For there shall arise false Christ's, and false prophets, and shall shew great signs and wonders; insomuch that, if it were possible, they shall deceive the very elect.*

Power- energeia- working, efficiency; in the New Testament used only of superhuman power, whether of God or of the Devil.

He comes with ALL, (means and types of) power (it will look the same as, the apostles ability) with signs and wonders; but it is all the working of Satan, as described in (**Revelation 13:13-17**). It's not a coincidence that in these last year's miracles have increased. While god still does miracles, it is this very thing that we are warned from Paul would deceive the people. Satan has often times disguised his false doctrines with supernatural signs. In today's open spiritual climate both inside and outside the Church. Our time is tailor-made for lying signs to deceive greater numbers of people than ever before. Experience becomes the teacher instead of the objective word of truth. What they think they see or hear of is always true to them.

(**2 Thessalonians 2:10**) *"And with all deceivableness of unrighteousness in them that perish; because they received not the love of the truth, that they might be saved."*

With all unrighteous deception among those who perish. The reason being, they did not receive the love of the truth that they might be saved.

(**2 Thessalonians 2:11**) *"And for this cause God shall send them strong delusion, that they should believe a lie?"*

For this reason God shall send them a STRONG delusion, and so they will believe the lie. They will be completely DECEIVED. God does not tell lies, only the truth. But in this instance he is going to allow their own lies to come to fruition, they will literally have to reject Gods counsel and step over the truth. They are brought to the point where they no longer even are able to consider the truth! Just as Pharaoh was given the chance to repent until he was deceived and empowered to fulfill God's will, likewise they will also. God sends them the lie through their own deception.

In the OT we find that God warned of false prophets through the true ones. But the people rejected God's true prophets so the Lord would allow a lying spirit in a prophet's mouth.

(**1 King 22:20-23**) *"And the LORD said, 'Who shall persuade Ahab that he may go up and fall at Ramothgilead?' And one said on this manner, and another said on that manner. And there came forth a spirit, and stood before the LORD, and said, I will persuade him. And the LORD said to him, wherewith? And he said, 'I will go forth and I will be a lying spirit in the mouth of all his prophets. And the he said thou shalt persuade him, and also prevail also: go forth, and do so. Now therefore, behold, the LORD hath put a lying spirit in the mouth of all thy prophets, and the LORD hath spoken evil concerning thee."*

Also found in (**2 Chronicles 18:21-22**).

God has often used the enemy to give people knowledge to see if they are for Him or against Him. (**Deuteronomy 13**) In the case of God sending a strong delusion it is not a test but for judgment because they have not believed the truth He will empower their lies. It is the church of Thiatira who allowed the false prophets inside, Jesus warns that they will be brought into the Great tribulation unless they repent.

(**Jeremiah 23:20-22**)*"The anger of the LORD shall not return, until he have executed, and till he have performed the thoughts of his heart: in the latter days ye shall consider it perfectly. I have not sent these prophets, yet they ran: I have not spoken to them, yet they prophesied. But if they had stood in my counsel, and had caused my people to hear my words, then they should have turned them from their evil way, and from the evil of their doings."*

The anger of the LORD will not turn back against these false prophets until he has performed and carried out the purposes of His heart. In the latter days you will understand it perfectly.

The ones who will be deceived by Satan and his counterfeit signs are those who have already rejected the truth. God will allow the deceiving spirits to speak through them without interfering.

(**2 Timothy 4:1**) *"I charge thee therefore before God, and the Lord Jesus Christ, who shall judge the quick and the dead at his appearing and his kingdom;"*

The example of the wickedness in Noah's day and the fact that life went on as usual, blinded them to impending destruction and is used to show that these lawless wicked men had a type of Tribulation judgment fall on them. Just like in Revelation. If certain churches do not repent they <u>will</u>

enter the Tribulation.

The Apostle Peters warns:

(**2 Peter 2:1-3**) *"But there were also false prophets among the people, even as there shall be false teachers among you, who privily shall bring in damnable heresies, even denying the Lord who bought them, and bring on themselves swift destruction. And many shall follow their pernicious ways; by reason of whom the way of truth shall be evil spoken of. And through covetousness shall they with feigned words of make merchandise of you: whose judgment now of a long time lingereth not, and their damnation slumbereth not."*

Notice the many and their way is destructive and their own destruction is close.

(**2 Thessalonians 2:12**) *"That they all might be damned who believed* (receive-hold to) *not the truth, but had pleasure in unrighteousness."*

The call for this salvation comes through the Gospel, the gospel Paul preached.

(**1 Corinthians 1:23**) *"But we preach Christ crucified, unto the Jews a stumbling block, and unto the Greeks foolishness;"*

It is this Gospel that we stand in and this Gospel that will enable us to obtain the glory of Jesus.

Instead they had pleasure in unrighteousness by doing it their way. They did not live in Christ's righteousness, or listen to His commands. They rejected them.

Most of the epistles were written to correct error; and Paul warned that error would accelerate after his death.

(**Acts 20:29**) *"For I know this that after my departing shall grievous wolves enter in among you, not sparing the flock."*

What had already begun in Paul's day finally comes to maturity in the end. The seeds that were planted by the enemy as tares has taken root and grown.

Shortly after Paul's martyrdom Jude said that false teachers had crept in unawares and therefore it was essential (as it still is today) to earnestly contend for the faith.

(**Jude 1:3-4**) *"Beloved, when I gave all diligence to write unto you of the common salvation, it was needful for me to write unto you, and exhort you that ye should earnestly contend for the faith which was once delivered unto the saints. For there are certain men* *crept in unawares, who were before of old ordained to this condemnation, ungodly men, turning the grace of our God into lasciviousness, and denying the only Lord God, and our Lord Jesus Christ.*"

The only question left to ask is: How much worse will the apostasy get before the Rapture and will you or I not become part of it?

If you now understand that all this is being fulfilled you might be wondering what then are we to do?

(**Luke 21:36**) "*Watch ye therefore, and pray always, that ye may be accounted worthy to escape all these things that shall come to pass, and to stand before the Son of Man.*"

(**1 John 3:2-3**) "*Beloved, now are we the sons of God, and it doth not yet appear what we shall be: but we know that, when he shall appear, we shall be like him; for we shall see him as he is. And every man that hath this hope in him purifieth himself, even as he is pure.*"

John had a glimpse in his vision he communicated in the book of revelation. He who has this hope looks forward to the Lord's return and purifies himself as Christ was pure. Come quickly Lord Jesus.

11 JUDGMENT AT THE HAND OF GOD

There is a level of evil that is building and sweeping across this nation as well as most of the world like never before. In all my years, I've never seen the level of wickedness and perversion as I see taking place currently in our world today. It's almost as if someone has flipped off the morality switch and all hell has broken loose.

Here are some points to consider

California is set to become the first State in the union that will require (mandate) every child in the State public school sector to know and learn about same sex relationships, homosexual lifestyles, tolerance/diversity training and, to top it all off, they (students) will be required to learn about homosexual "civil rights" leaders such as Harvey Milk.

Not only has California fought long and hard to make this a political issue, even the Obama Administration is watching this closely, as they to, are designing a program which will bring homosexual diversity training into the classroom to children as young as 5 years of age.

Then, with the recent passage and signing into law of New York becoming the 6th State in the union to adopt gay marriage, the recent lifting of the ban on homosexuals in the military and President Obama himself stating his views of gay marriage is "evolving", the nation is spinning out of control and perversion is becoming another form of normalcy in the land.

Senators and Congressmen caught in the act of immorality, television preachers caught in love triangles while continuing to make millions off of un-discerning supporters. There is a foul spirit in the air and it's growing.

Recently, statements by Washington officials and political insiders that suggest the real possibility of civil unrest in this nation are prompting many officials to consider enforcing martial law if things come to a head. It seems our nation is heading toward a point of no return.

From catastrophic weather events where floods, tornados and the past harsh winter where national records for snow and cold temperatures were broken, homes destroyed, lives taken and virtual communities lost forever, all suggest something is happening in our land.

Immorality seems to now be the rule of the day, where open nudity can be seen almost everywhere, where even the push for the secularization of children seems to be epidemic and the idea of traditional morality is seen as repressive and out of date, we are sacrificing whatever morality we have left on the altar of idolatry.

The world is being shaken. From the economic turmoil that control the economic destiny of people everywhere, to the regulation of restrictions against Christians in democratic nations such as Canada and the UK, where it is now illegal for a preacher to declare the word of God against sin, especially when it comes to homosexuality. Preachers as well as Pastors are being jailed for doing nothing more than proclaiming the truth.

Even in the church today, immorality, false teachings and idol worship is gaining a foothold in many pulpits across America. What was once preached against has now become accepted, and what is now accepted is being preached to those who have ears to listen and hearts to believe. A form of Godliness is all too common today and yet, most believe they are experiencing a revival, yet there is no true power behind it.

It seems as though someone has taken all of the worse case scenarios one could dream up and found a way to make it reality. Even in our civil laws, where justice is promised to the weak and the abused, justice is but an illusion to the highest bidder or the best looking. When a mother, accused of murdering her child can be acquitted by a jury for murdering her own child; who sought the life of night clubs, who waited almost one month before reporting her child missing, as in the case of Casey Anthony, there is a problem with our culture. The Justice system itself has become just that, just-a-system.

But these events, these occurrences are indicators that our world is on a collision course with judgment. With each new day that brings another amazing revelation or discovery, or catastrophe, it only proves one thing, that our world is coming to a significant point in time where Christ has all but told us would come in due season. Today's headlines are reading like the very pages of Revelation and as such, our only thought should be as believers is, are we doing all we can to preach the gospel before the end of our age nears?

So what is happening? What is going on in our world? Obviously the world is not getting better, it's becoming worse and with every passing moment of time. What is the answer? The answer lies in the words of Jesus himself in (**Matthew 24**), where he spoke about signs in the heavens as well as in the earth. Jesus gave us a warning of what was to come, and by the looks of it, his words of warning are echoing true.

We as Christians need to take an account where we are at in our own lives, for the time is coming when those around us will not endure sound doctrine, but instead, seeking soothing words, and will seek false words and a false hope. But I will move forward, preaching to all those who will hear, that judgment is coming.

(**2 Timothy 3:1-5**) *"But know this: There will be terrible times in the last days. People will be lovers of themselves, lovers of money, boastful, proud, abusive, disobedient to their parents, ungrateful, unholy, without love, unforgiving, slanderous, without self-control, brutal, not lovers of the good, treacherous, rash, conceited, lovers of pleasure rather than lovers of God, having a form of godliness but denying its power. Have nothing to do with such people."*

Repent, for the judgment of God is at hand.

What Does the Bible Say About God's Judgment? God has always existed as judge over His creation. But we need to understand how He judges, when He judges and why He judges.

Knowing how, when and why He judges helps us understand the kinds of judgment described in the Bible.

When God determined to punish Sodom and Gomorrah for their sins, Abraham recognized that God is the judge of men's actions.

(**Genesis 18:20-25**) *"And the LORD said, Because the cry of Sodom and Gomorrah is great, and because their sin is very grievous; I will go down now, and see whether they have done altogether according to the cry of it, which is come unto me; and if not, I will know. And the men turned their faces from thence, and went toward Sodom: but Abraham stood yet before the LORD. And Abraham drew near, and said, Wilt thou also destroy the righteous with the wicked? Peradventure there be fifty righteous within the city: wilt thou also destroy and not spare the place for the fifty righteous that are therein? That be far from thee to do after this manner, to slay the righteous with the wicked: and that the righteous should be as the wicked, that be far from thee: Shall not the Judge of all the earth do right?"*

In this case God passed judgment, issued a verdict and carried out the sentence.

(**Psalm 75:7**) *"But God is the judge: he putteth down one, and sitteth up another. Declares, "But God is the Judge; He puts down one, and exalts another."*

Nebuchadnezzar came to understand this.

(**Daniel 4:37**) *"Now I Nebuchadnezzar praise and extol and honor the King of heaven, all whose works are truth, and his ways judgment: and those that walk in pride he is able to abase."*

And Daniel passed on this truth to the blasphemous Belshazzar

(**Daniel 5:21-22**) *"And he was driven from the sons of men; and his heart was made like the beasts, and his dwelling was with the wild asses: they fed him with grass like oxen, and his body was wet with the dew of heaven; till he knew that the most high God ruled in the kingdom of men, and that he appointeth over it whomsoever he will. And thou his son, O Belshazzar, hast not humbled thine heart, though thou knewest all this;"*

In these cases God is not judging people to determine their suitability to receive salvation, nor is God making right every injustice. These instances show that God will intervene, however, to deal with injustices or sin for the benefit of mankind and to further His purposes. Judgment is not passed on the majority of people now in this age for the purpose of eternal salvation. This kind of judgment will occur later. Jude tells us that.

(**Jude 1:14-15**) *"And Enoch also, the seventh from Adam, prophesied of these, saying, Behold, the Lord cometh with ten thousands of His saints to execute judgment on all, and to convince all that are ungodly among them of all their ungodly deeds which they have ungodly committed, and of all their hard speeches which ungodly sinners have spoken against him."*

God's ultimate purpose for man is that he will enjoy eternal life in the family of God. Since God is not calling everyone now.

(**John 6:65**) *"And he said, therefore said I unto you, that no man can come unto me, except it were given unto him of my Father."*

He is not judging every person now to grant or deny him eternal life.

(**John 12:47-48**) *"And if any man hear my words, and believe not, I judge him not: for I came not to judge the world, but to save the world. He that rejecteth me, and receiveth not my words, hath one that judgeth him: the word that I have spoken, the same shall judge him in the last day."*

God reserves this kind of judgment for humans until later, when they will fully grasp God's truth as it is presented to them. Only then can they be fairly judged on the basis of that truth. God will not hold people accountable for what they don't know. Sin, however, is always judged to be worthy of death.

(**Romans 6:23**) *"For the wages of sin is death; but the gift of God is eternal life through Jesus Christ our Lord."*

And therefore the whole world is guilty before God.

(**Romans 3:19**) *"Now we know that what things soever the law saith, it saith to them who are under the law: that every mouth may be stopped, and all the world may become guilty before God."*

And death is upon all because of their sin.

(**Romans 5:12**) *"Wherefore, as by one man sin entered into the world, and death by sin; and so death passed upon all men, for that all have sinned:"*

(**Hebrews 8:8-12**) *"For finding fault with them, he saith, Behold, the days come, saith the Lord, when I will make a new covenant with the house of Israel and with the house of Judah: Not according to the covenant that I made with their fathers in the day when I took them by the hand to lead them out of the land of Egypt; because they continued not in my covenant, and I regarded them not, saith the Lord. For this is the covenant that I will make with the house of Israel after those days, saith the Lord; I will put my laws into their mind, and write them in their hearts: and I will be to them a God, and they shall be to me a people: And they shall not teach every man his neighbor, and every man his brother, saying, Know the Lord: for all shall know me, from the least to the greatest. For I will be merciful to their unrighteousness, and their sins and their iniquities will I remember no more."*

This speaks of a time yet future during which people who are unaware of God's truth will be brought into a new covenant with God, and then they will all know God, and their sins will be forgiven.

The judgment of God is also described in the Bible as a process, not strictly the rendering of a verdict or passing of a sentence. For example, Peter tells us that *"the time has come for judgment to begin at the house of God"*

(**1 Peter 4:17**) *"For the time is come that judgment must begin at the house of God: and if it first begin at us, what shall the end be of them that obey not the gospel of God?"*

From this we can see that judgment is an evaluation process that has already begun for those who are a part of God's Church-"the house of God." This evaluation ultimately leads to a rendering of a decision or verdict.

Some of Jesus' parables illustrate that judgment is a process that eventually leads to a decision and a reward or lack thereof. The parables of the pounds.

(**Luke 19:12-27**) *"He said therefore, A certain nobleman went into a far country to receive for himself a kingdom, and to return. And he called his ten servants, and delivered them ten pounds, and said unto them, Occupy till I come. But his citizens hated him, and sent a message after him, saying, we will not have this man to reign over us. And it came to pass, that when he was returned, having received the kingdom, then he commanded these servants to be called unto him, to whom he had given the money, that he might know how much every man had gained by trading. Then came the first, saying, Lord, thy pound hath gained ten pounds. And he said unto him, Well, thou good servant: because thou hast been faithful in a very little, have thou authority over ten cities. And the second came, saying, Lord, thy pound hath gained five pounds. And he said likewise to him, be thou also over five cities. And another came, saying, Lord, behold, here is thy pound, which I have kept laid up in a napkin: For I feared thee, because thou art an austere man: thou takest up that thou layedst not down, and reapest that thou didst not sow. And he saith unto him, Out of thine own mouth will I judge thee, thou wicked servant. Thou knewest that I was an austere man, taking up that I laid not down, and reaping that I did not sow: Wherefore then gavest not thou my money into the bank, that at my coming I might have required mine own with usury? And he said unto them that stood by, Take from him the pound, and give it to him that hath ten pounds. And they said unto him, Lord, he hath ten pounds. For I say unto you, that unto every one which hath shall be given; and from him that hath not, even that he hath shall be taken away from him. But those mine enemies, which would not that I should reign over them, bring hither, and slay them before me."*

Talents

(**Matthew 25:14-30**) *"For the kingdom of heaven is as a man travelling into a far country, who called his own servants, and delivered unto them his goods. And unto one he gave five talents, to another two, and to another one; to every man according to his several ability; and straightway took his journey. Then he that had received the five talents went and traded with the same, and made them other five talents. And likewise he that had received two, he also gained other two. But he that had received one went and digged in the earth, and hid his lord's money. After a long time the lord of those servants cometh, and reckoneth with them. And so he that had received five talents came and brought other five talents, saying, Lord, thou deliveredst unto me five talents: behold, I have gained beside them five talents more. His lord said unto him, well done, thou good and faithful servant: thou hast been faithful over a few things, I will make thee ruler over many things: enter thou into the joy of thy lord. He also that had received two talents came and said, Lord, thou deliveredst unto me two talents: behold, I have gained two other talents beside them. His lord said unto him, well done, good and faithful servant; thou hast been faithful over* *a few things, I will make thee ruler over many things: enter thou into the joy of thy lord. Then he which had received the one talent came and said, Lord, I knew thee that thou art an hard man, reaping where thou hast not sown, and gathering where thou hast not strawed: And I was afraid, and went and hid thy talent in the earth: lo, there thou hast that is thine. His lord answered and said unto him, Thou wicked and slothful servant, thou knewest that I reap where I sowed not, and gather where I have not strawed: Thou oughtest therefore to have put my money to the exchangers, and then at my coming I should have received mine own with usury. Take therefore the talent from him, and give it unto him which hath ten talents. For unto every one that hath shall be given, and he shall have abundance: but from him that hath not shall be taken away even that which he hath. And cast ye the unprofitable servant into outer darkness: there shall be weeping and gnashing of teeth."*

Laborers in the vineyard

(**Matthew 20:1-16**) *"For the kingdom of heaven is like unto a man that is an householder, which went out early in the morning to hire laborers into his vineyard. And when he had agreed with the laborers for a penny a day, he sent them into his vineyard. And he went out about the third hour, and saw others standing idle in the marketplace, and said unto them; Go ye also into the vineyard, and whatsoever is right I will give you. And they went their way. Again he went out about the sixth and ninth hour, and did likewise. And about the eleventh hour he went out, and found others standing idle, and saith unto them, Why stand ye here all the day idle? They say unto him, because no man hath hired us. He saith unto them, Go ye also into the vineyard; and whatsoever is right, that shall ye receive. So when even was come, the lord of the vineyard saith unto his steward, Call the laborers, and give them their hire, beginning from the last unto the first. And when they came that were hired about the eleventh hour, they received every man a penny. But when the first came, they supposed that they should have received more; and they likewise received every man a penny. And when they had received it, they murmured against the Goodman of the house, Saying, These last have wrought but one hour, and thou hast made them equal unto us, which have borne the burden and heat of the day. But he answered one of them, and said, Friend, I do thee no wrong: didst not thou agree with me for a penny? Take that thine is, and go thy way: I will give unto this last, even as unto thee. Is it not lawful for me to do what I will with mine own? Is thine eye evil, because I am good? So the last shall be first, and the first last: for many be called, but few chosen."*

10 virgins

(**Matthew 25:1-13**) *"Then shall the kingdom of heaven be likened unto ten virgins, which took their lamps, and went forth to meet the bridegroom. And five of them were wise, and five were foolish. They that were foolish took their lamps, and took no oil with them: But the wise took oil in their vessels with their lamps. While the bridegroom* *tarried, they all slumbered and slept. And at midnight there was a cry made, Behold, the bridegroom cometh; go ye out to meet him. Then all those virgins arose, and trimmed their lamps. And the foolish said unto the wise, give us of your oil; for our lamps are gone out. But the wise answered, saying, not so; lest there be not enough for us and you: but go ye rather to them that sell, and buy for yourselves. And while they went to buy, the bridegroom came; and they that were ready went in with him to the marriage: and the door was shut. Afterward came also the other virgins, saying, Lord, Lord, open to us. But he answered and said, Verily I say unto you, I know you not. Watch therefore, for ye know neither the day nor the hour wherein the Son of man cometh."*

All help to clarify that judgment is a process after which comes a reckoning. During the Millennium, God will judge people on how they live during that time; the 1,000 years will be a period during which God holds all people accountable.

(**Revelation 20:4**) *"And I saw thrones, and they sat upon them, and judgment was given unto them: and I saw the souls of them that were beheaded for the witness of Jesus, and for the word of God, and which had not worshipped the beast, neither his image, neither had received his mark upon their foreheads, or in their hands; and they lived and reigned with Christ a thousand years."*

After this evaluation process, we will be judged according to our works.

(**Revelation 22:12**) *"And, behold, I come quickly; and my reward is with me, to give every man according as his work shall be."*

There will be a reckoning only after a fair and ample process is complete.

(**Matthew 25:31-34**) *"When the Son of man shall come in his glory, and all the holy angels with him, then shall he sit upon the throne of his glory: And before him shall be gathered all nations: and he shall separate them one from another, as a shepherd divideth his sheep from the goats: And he shall set the sheep on his right hand, but the goats on the left. Then shall the King say unto them on his right hand, Come, ye blessed of my Father, inherit the kingdom prepared for you from the foundation of the world."*

When you really turn to God, you can confidently ask Him to step into your life in a powerful way. How God deals with you to fulfill His purpose in you is described in the Bible as a form of His "judgments." When God is intimately involved in your life, He makes decisions about you daily. His decisions about us have to do with answers to our prayers, bestowing His blessings on us, protecting us and even allowing us to endure trials. God is deeply interested in us and how we are progressing toward fulfilling His purpose.

David saw God's judgments in all His works and recognized that they were apparent throughout the creation.

(**Psalm 105:5**) *"Remember his marvelous works that he hath done; his wonders, and the judgments of his mouth;"*

David knew all God's decisions regarding him were right and in his best interest. Therefore David praised God continually for His faithful judgments in his life.

(**Psalm 119:20**) *"My soul breaketh for the longing that it hath unto thy judgments at all times."*

God, the Judge over all creation, makes decisions. It is in His power to decide-and carry out-righteous and merciful judgments. We can be confident that God is a righteous judge.

(**Psalm 7:11**) *"God judgeth the righteous, and God is angry with the wicked every day."*

(**2 Timothy 4:8**) *"Henceforth there is laid up for me a crown of righteousness, which the Lord, there righteous judge, shall give me at that day: and not to me only, but unto all them also that love his appearing."*

Judgment day

The apostle Paul was one of God's most faithful servants. And I believe there were three important motivations behind Paul's faithfulness: hope, love--and fear. Paul had a blessed hope of eternal life that motivated him to faithfulness. He also had a great love for Christ. In (**2 Corinthians 5:14**) he says, "*The love of Christ constraineth us*"- meaning, it constrained him to remain faithful to God.

But Paul's faithfulness was also motivated by something else: the reverential fear of the hour he would stand before the Judge of the world-- on Judgment Day!

Today, the vast majority of Christians possess only the first two motivations. Virtually every believer claims to have the hope of eternal life. And many say in all sincerity, "I know I love Jesus with all my heart."

But what is missing in the church of Jesus Christ in these last days is that third motivation--the awesome sense that one day we will stand before a holy God and give an account of our every motive thought and action. We seldom, if ever, think of that Day of Judgment!

Yet the truth of a coming day of judgment is the very thing that produces serious, godly believers. Those who put it out of mind are usually cold, careless and indulgent. But the fact remains that. Sometime very soon, every person who has ever lived will be gathered to the place of judgment-- to be judged by Jesus Christ:

(**2 Corinthians 5:10**) "*For we must all appear before the judgment seat of Christ.*"

(**Romans 14:12**) "*So then every one of us shall give account of himself to God.*"

At this very moment, legions of angels stand ready for Jesus' command to gather from the corners of the earth both the wicked and the righteous:

(**Matthew 13:41**) "*The Son of man shall send forth his angels, and they shall gather out of his kingdom all things that offend, and them which do iniquity.*"

All the rich, famous and powerful of all ages will be brought to stand before Him:

(**Revelation 6:15-17**) "*And the kings of the earth, and the great men, and the rich men, and the chief captains, and the mighty men...hid themselves in the dens and in the rocks of the mountains; and said to the mountains and the rocks, Fall on us, hide us from the face of him that sitteth on the throne, and from the wrath of the Lamb: for the great day of his wrath is come; and who shall be able to stand?*"

A famous actress is constantly talking about reincarnation. She claims she has lived many lives before, and that when she dies she'll come back to earth in another body.

What terror awaits her and her followers! An angel of the Lord will be sent to their grave sites, uniting body and soul-and they will suddenly discover there is not another life! Instead, they will be summoned by the Judge to the last court--a court of no appeals. And the only afterlife will be eternal damnation for all who rejected Him.

Indeed, the angels will gather together all the "tares"--the sinners and the ungodly--and drag them "*in bundles to burn them*". (**Matthew 13:40, 30**) These will not come willingly, but with weeping, wailing and gnashing of teeth.

God Has Been Keeping Books on Every Living Soul Since Adam. God has recorded every passion and motive of every person--every single thought, word and deed. The motives of the Christian are entered in a "book of remembrance," which is the Book of Life. And on the Day of Judgment, Christ is going to remember all who are in this book:

(**Malachi 3:16-17**) "*Then they that feared the Lord spake often to one another: and the Lord...heard it, and a book of remembrance was written before him for them that feared the Lord.... And they shall be mine, saith the Lord of hosts, in that day when I make up my jewels; and I will spare them, as a man spareth his own son that serveth him*".

If you love Jesus with all your heart and you're cleansed by His blood. Then your name is written in His book of remembrance. Such need not fear this message; in fact, it should bring great rejoicing to your heart as you see all that God has planned for those who love Him!

But there is the Book--and there are books. The Bible says each life has its own book, a record of an entire lifetime on earth:

(**Revelation 20: 11-13**) "*And I saw a great white throne, and him that sat on it, from whose face the earth and the heaven fled away.... And I saw the dead, small and great, stand before God; and the books were opened...and the dead were judged out of those things which were written in the books, according to their works. And the sea gave up the dead which were in it; and death and hell delivered up the dead which were in them: and they were judged according to their works*".

The wicked and ungodly will be judged by everything written in those books- one by one. Before the judge of all!

Scripture says every person will have a resurrection body at that time. The sinner will have a body 'fitted to destruction". (**Romans 9:22**) But the godly will be given a new body, likened unto the Lord's! And when the judgment is over, the Lamb will rise up from His throne and lead His flock into eternal paradise.

Yet before the Judge does this, He will beckon us by His side as He judges the wicked:

(**Revelation 3:21**) "*To him that overcometh will I grant to sit with me in my throne, even as I also overcame, and am set down with my Father in his throne.*"

Jesus is going to say to us, "Come--sit at my right hand as the judgments proceed!"

Try to Imagine the Scene That Takes Place as the Judgment Begins Hitler cringes in agony as the Judge tells His angels to read the roll-call of names of every Jew he murdered. Six million names--those of every man, woman and child he killed! Every scream will be replayed, every cry from the ovens heard again. All his henchmen will share his terror.

Next comes the army of abortion doctors and nurses, huddled together before the Judge. They listen and shudder as the names of millions of babies are read. God has a name for every one-because according to the

Scriptures they were named from eternity see (**Jeremiah 1:5**).

Every scream from the womb will be replayed--and the doctors who performed those murderous acts will have to stand and endure each cry. Every mother who allowed her baby to be killed will be shown the life God planned for her child-and how her baby was robbed of that life. The Judge will expose it all!

Then there are those who "*neglected their salvation*" see (**Hebrews 2:3**). They stand in great shock, not believing they are numbered with the transgressors. Listen to their cries:

(**Isaiah 64:6**) "*But we are all as an unclean thing, and all our righteousness's are as filthy rags; and we all do fade as a leaf; and our iniquities, like the wind, have taken us away.*"

An angel will stand among them, repeating to them the Scriptures they heard during their lifetime:

(**Hebrews 2:1**) "*You gave no earnest heed to the things which you heard.*"

(**Hebrews 2:3**) "*How do you hope to escape, seeing you have neglected so great a salvation, which was so clearly revealed and confirmed to you?*"

Yet here they all are before the judgment seat, bundled together in one group-paralyzed with agony and fear! It is the day of God's wrath and vengeance. And now, as each book is opened and every vile deed voiced aloud, what has become of their bluster? Where now are the bold blasphemies, the mockery of sacred things? Where is their cry?

Scripture declares, "*The ungodly shall not stand in the judgment*" (**Psalm 1:5**) Look now at the others trembling before the judgment seat: Judges who allowed unborn babies to be murdered. Atheistic college professors who filled a whole generation full of apostasy and hate for Christ. Lying politicians who removed prayer and God from our society. Godless presidents, dictators and mob leaders. Actors and filmmakers who blasphemed Christ. Artists who depicted His Cross in a vat of urine. Bankers, business people, the rich, the once proud and powerful that had no time for Him. Now what will they do?

There they stand, listening and awaiting their turn. And the angel of the Lord cries out among them," *Be sure your sin will find you out!*" (**Numbers 32:23**)

The Judge Will Call Forth Witnesses!

The Judge, Jesus Christ, is faithful-and He will call forth His witnesses.

These will testify either for you or against you. The first witness is the Word of God itself:

(**John 12:48**) "*He that rejecteth me, and receiveth not my words, hath one that judgeth him: the word that I have spoken, the same shall judge him in the last day.*"

For every sermon or gospel song ever heard, every Bible verse or tract ever read, account must be given. Jesus says, "Every word I have spoken to you will judge you on that day. My Word will be the witness!"

Witnesses shall arise such as the men of Nineveh, the men of Sodom and the Queen of Sheba.

(**Matthew 12:41-42**) "*The men of Nineveh shall rise in judgment with this generation, and shall condemn it: because they repented at the preaching of Jonas: and, behold, a greater than Jonas is here. The queen of the south shall rise up in the judgment with this generation, and shall condemn it: for she came from the uttermost parts of the earth to hear the wisdom of Solomon; and, behold, a greater than Solomon is here.*"

When you stand before the Judge and your book is opened, the vast multitudes of Ninevites will step forward. Those who died in the holocaust of Sodom and Gomorrah will come forth, as will those of Tyre and Sidon. These wicked ones will gather round, incredulous as they hear the list of all the opportunities you had to receive the Word of God: Bibles, radio, and TV, teachers, witnesses, and friends, family.

They will cry out, "This man's judgment ought to be worse than ours! How could he reject so many opportunities and deny such powerful light? We had no Bible, no constant reminders, no second opportunity. But he had all this!"

Jesus says Sodom would have repented if they had heard what you've heard.

(**Matthew 11:23**) "*For if the mighty works, which have been done in thee, had been done in Sodom, it would have remained until this day.*"

The men of Sodom would have put on sackcloth and ashes if they'd heard even a fraction of the gospel preaching you have heard! Preachers and pastors will be called forth as witnesses.

(**Matthew 24: 14**) "*This gospel of the kingdom shall be preached in all the world for a witness unto all nations.*"

We shepherds will have to stand and bear witness that you were in attendance in the house of God. You heard the witness of the gospel preached. And we must affirm before the Judge of all people every truth you heard--either for you or against you!

Perhaps the Most Tragic Souls Standing Before the Judge Will Be Those the Bible Calls "Unprofitable Servants."

These were the servants--meaning, they called themselves by the name of the Lord.

You see, the unprofitable servant" is the one who "hid" his talent. He was too lazy to invest his life and time in God's interests, and he became "slothful" in the things of God. This was the busy man or woman who came to God's house once a week to keep a semblance of religion.

Yet here is what the Lord will say of haphazard, halfhearted service to Him:

(**Matthew 25:26-27, 30**)"*Thou wicked and slothful servant thou knewest that I reap where I sowed not...Thou oughtest therefore to have put my money to the exchangers, and then at my coming I should have received mine own with (interest).... Cast ye the unprofitable servant into outer darkness: there shall be weeping and gnashing of teeth*".

What weeping and wailing there will be when the unprofitable servant's book is opened! The Judge will show the world how much time and effort he spent in making money, seeking personal security, building up bank accounts, fretting, ignoring family, forgetting God and forsaking the assembly of believers.

On that day God will bring forth the record of every neglected church meeting, every lazy and self-centered activity. Then, right before this servant's eyes will appear everything he spent his lifetime accumulating: houses, cars, furnishings, boats, clothes, jewelry, stocks and bonds.

Suddenly, a spark leaps from the Judge's eye--the spark of a Lover who has been shunned--and it ignites everything like a hydrogen meltdown! Standing before the Judge is an angel, and in the angel's hands is a mound of dust. The Lord will turn to the unprofitable one and say, "This is what your lifetime of business amounted to! I needed you and called you, but you neglected me. You gave me so little of your time, until finally you pushed me out of your life completely. You wasted your life for a handful of dust-yet you were warned it would all burn as grass in an oven!"

Oh, the regret there will be on that day for a man who has no time for God now! He attends the obligatory Sunday morning service with his wife and children, because it's "the American way." But he has no heart for God! You never see him in a prayer meeting or enjoying the true fellowship of the saints, encouraging and being encouraged in the Lord, as the Word commands.

Yet on Judgment Day, the Judge will say, take that unprofitable servant and cast him out of my presence! His heart is not with me; it never has been. He left his first love long ago. He has not made me the Lover of his soul. Otherwise, in every waking hour I would have been on his mind--in his business, his family, all his doings. He would have put my interests first in everything!"

Oh. Who will not be afraid on that at Day of Judgment?

What Does Judgment Day Mean for the Overcoming Children of God?

The first thing on the Judge's agenda will be to separate His sheep from among the goats. He will not allow His righteous ones to be numbered with the transgressors. Instead, He will call on His angels to gather His flock at His right hand:

(**Matthew 25:32-34**)"*And before him shall be gathered all nations: and he shall separate them one from another, as a shepherd divideth his sheep from the goats: and he shall set the sheep on his right hand, but the goats on the left. Then shall the King say unto them on his right hand, Come, ye blessed of my Father, inherit the kingdom prepared for you from the foundation of the world*".

The Bible is very clear that those who have been abiding in Christ and looking for His appearing will have boldness and confidence on that day:

(**1 John 2:28**) "*And now, little children, abide in him; that, when he shall appear, we may have confidence, and not be ashamed before him at his coming*".

(**1 John 4: 17**) "*Herein is our love made perfect, that we may have boldness in the day of judgment: because as he is, so are we in this world*".

How can you have such boldness on the Day of Judgment--such joy and confidence? It comes only through knowing the Judge--as your friend, brother, redeemer-kinsman, Lord, high priest, propitiation, advocate, intercessor, and the love of your heart--your very life!

There is a test that will show whether or not you are prepared to go to the judgment as a sheep--with joy, confidence and boldness. The Bible says.

(**1 Corinthians 11:31**) "*For if we would judge ourselves, we should not be judged.*"

Are you willing to take the test--and to judge yourself? If you are willing, ask yourself these three questions:

1. Have you been longing and yearning for the coming of the Lord?

2. Do you look forward to His coming?
3. Do you yearn for the day when He will appear?

(**Titus 2:13**) "*Looking for that blessed hope, and the glorious appearing of the great God and our Savior Jesus Christ*"

(**2 Timothy 4:8**) "*Henceforth there is laid up for me a crown of righteousness, which the Lord, the righteous judge, shall give me at that day: and not to me only, but unto all them also that love his appearing*"

This world is not our home. But I ask you: Are you putting down roots? Or are you pulling up roots, praying, "Jesus, keep my heart awake!"

(**2 Peter 3:12, 14**) "*Looking for and hasting unto the coming of the day of God.... Wherefore, beloved, seeing that ye look for such things, be diligent that ye may be found of him in peace, without spot, and blameless*".

Jesus said, "*Occupy till I come*" (**Luke 19:13**). We all must go ahead with our daily lives and work. But in every waking hour, our hearts should cry, "*Even so, come, Lord Jesus!*" (**Revelation 22:20**)

Have God's enemies become your enemies? Are you engaged in the battle against those who oppose God? Have you taken up His fight against the flesh, the world and the devil? Or have you left the battle in the hands of other members of Christ's body?

If you're going to stand before the world and judge God's enemies on Judgment Day, you have to make them your enemies now. David said.

(**Psalm 139:21-22**) "*Do not I hate them, O Lord, that hate thee? And am not I grieved with those that rise up against thee? I hate them with a perfect hatred: I count them mine enemies.*"

Yes, Jesus said we are to love our enemies. But what about His enemies-those who hate Him, refuse His grace and mercy, and defame His name and drag it through filth? We are not to hate men-but we are to hate the sin that is in their hearts and the demonic powers that rule them. We are to hate the wickedness that is in the world!

Yet do you say in your heart, "This world has been wicked all along, and it's only going to get worse. But what concern is that to me? I'll just keep my garment clean before God." NO--YOU CAN'T! We are all in a battle, in warfare! The gates of hell are coming against the church of Jesus Christ in these last days like never before-and you cannot remain neutral! God issues a call:

(**Psalms 94:16**) "*Who will rise up for me against the evildoers?*"

And when Judgment Day comes, I want to say with Paul, "I fought a good fight!" I want to go out fighting--to be on my knees, full of holy hatred toward sin in my life and in the world. Have you not made a habit of forsaking the house of God?

(**Hebrews 10:25**) "*Not forsaking the assembling of ourselves together, as the manner of some is; but exhorting one another: and so much the more, as ye see the day approaching.*"

It is no accident that the very next verse in this passage refers to "willful sinning" after the truth has been revealed. Indeed, it is a proven historical fact: People become most careless and neglectful just prior to judgment and calamity!

Always before any society spun completely out of control, people turned to security, money-making, pleasures--everything but God. And at the last moment, things got worse: Believers began neglecting the house of God. Paul warns us: Now that the day is approaching so soon, make sure you do not forsake the assembling of yourselves together, as so many have done! This is no time to drift or to stay away from God's house. It is time to assemble with true overcomers!

If you're church on Sundays is nothing more than a TV program, then beloved. You are not assembling with believers you are not getting or giving encouragement. As God commands!

What is the judgment, but the final assembling together of His flock? Will you be there--faithful, expectant, willing and joyful? The Lord knows those who love Him so much they can't stand to be away from His body. I tell you, the books will be opened on that day--and the Judge is keeping an account right now!

Did You Pass the Test?

If you know in your heart you're not ready to stand before Jesus--and that time is coming very soon--then you have to answer for what I have written here. This one message is enough to damn you to eternal hell if you reject it. It will stand as a witness on Judgment Day!

Have your interests--your work, your possessions or even your ministry--become more important to you than the Lord's interests? Have you neglected your family? Are you satisfied because you go to church on Sunday and say, I've done my part for God"? God's Word to you is clear: It's not enough!

If you have judged yourself and come up short, then pray this from your heart: that the LORD God will forgive you.

Then End

ABOUT THE AUTHOR

I live in the southeast and have been serving in the ministry of the Lord for many years. I have seen the Church go thou much change over the years. One night in prayer I went to the Lord and complained about the things that I was seeing start to take place in the Church. Much to my surprise He told me to write about it, I might say that I never have thought about writing before that. Since then I have written a lot and have many book in the works now, and plan on writing till He tells me to stop.

Made in the USA
Lexington, KY
31 October 2016